D0350633

William Faulkner

M. Thomas Inge is the Robert Emory Blackwell Professor of English and the Humanities at Randolph-Macon College. The author or editor of more than fifty books, including *Conversations with William Faulkner* and the *Handbook on American Popular Culture*, Inge has lectured abroad in eighteen countries. He lives in Ashland, Virginia.

William
Faulkner

M. Thomas Inge

OVERLOOK DUCKWORTH

NEW YORK • WOODSTOCK • LONDON

Acknowledgments

Without the magisterial editions of Joseph Blotner's *Faulkner: A Biography* (1974 and 1984), other dependable biographies of William Faulkner would not be possible. Blotner's thorough documentation and his ability to dispel myth and rumor in favor of fact have enabled other biographers to follow their own personal agendas and theories without losing sight of the real Faulkner behind the icon, or as much of the real Faulkner as we are likely ever to know. I did meet Faulkner on one occasion, and he patiently answered a few questions.

My understanding of Faulkner's work has been greatly enriched over the past forty years not only by Blotner but through conversations with colleagues and fellow Faulknerians, such as Ann J. Abadie, John E. Bassett, William Boozer, Cleanth Brooks, Sergei Chakovsky, Hunter Cole, Martha E. Cook, Doreen Fowler, Michel Gresset, Robert W. Hamblin, Lothar Honnighausen, John Lowe, Thomas McHaney, David Minter, Mo Yan, Paul A. Orlov, Ladell Payne, Charles A. Peek, Francois Pitavy, Noel Polk, Carl E. Rollyson, Jr., Judith Sensibar, Dorothy Scura, Tao Jie, Joan Williams, Thomas Daniel Young, and Waldemar Zacharasiewicz. To anyone I have inadvertently omitted from this alphabetical list, my apologies.

The visual documentation of Faulkner's life has been greatly facilitated by the rich collections of photographs and illustrations at the University of Mississippi Library, Special Collections, Southern Media Archive (Jennifer Aronson, Curator of Visual Collections); and the University of Virginia Library, Special Collections (Michael Plunkett, Director of Special Collections). Both have been helpfully cooperative, as have other owners of visual materials, including Mary Ann Connell, William Boozer, Glennray Tutor, Graham S. Frear, Richard Thompson, and Rick Geary, the last four artists without peers.

A special word of thanks is due my friend Ruth Prigozy who recommended me for this project. If only Stan were still here. The administrators at Randolph-Macon College, especially Dean Robert K. Holyer and President Roger Martin, have been unfailingly supportive on this and other projects.   Two grants from the Walter Williams Craigie Teaching Endowment, administered by the Committee on Faculty Development, have substantially and materially made the writing and production of this book possible. Donária provides the rhythm and inspiration.

—M. Thomas Inge

> *"I will have to hunt up somebody ... who will stop anybody making*
> *the Wm Faulkner story the moment I have breathed my last."*
> —Letter to Harold Ober, August, 1958 (*Letters* 415).

Few modern writers influenced the shape and nature of twentieth-century fiction more profoundly than William Faulkner. James Joyce is usually cited as Faulkner's exemplar in the art of writing fiction, but they actually share only superficial similarities: the use of local or regional experience as subject matter, the unconventional and experimental structure of their novels, and a playful way with words beyond their service in traditional communication.

Faulkner wrote as if there were no literature written in English before him, no century and more of convention and literary tradition established before he put pen to paper. He recreated fiction anew and set the novel free to better serve the twentieth century through a powerful, discordant, and irresistible torrent of language that crashed through time, space, and experience to tell the story of modern mankind in ways both tragic and comic. Faulkner would have written the way he did whether or not James Joyce, Virginia Woolf, Joseph Conrad, and the others had ever existed.

His life was as distinctive as his work. Unlike F. Scott Fitzgerald, who sampled a Princeton education and cast his lot among the wealthy and sophisticated, Faulkner had no certificate, diploma, or degree to add to his name and scorned education to spend his time among the dirt farmers and hunting companions in rural Mississippi. Unlike Ernest Hemingway, who learned to write through journalism and self-discipline and cast himself on the world stage as an adventurer and great white hunter, Faulkner studied and borrowed from all the great writers who preceded him and disappeared into his study shunning the popularity and gaze of the world at large. "One day I seemed to shut a door between me and all publishers' addresses and book lists," he recalled when beginning to write *The Sound and the Fury.* "I said to myself; Now I can write" *(Essays* 299).

He was more like Thomas Wolfe, whose flow of words filled trunks with manuscript pages so copiously that several editors had to reshape them into novels. But Faulkner was able to impose structure and order on his abundant prose to create remarkably multifaceted works of the imagination. He admired Wolfe more than Fitzgerald and Hemingway, he once said, because "Wolfe made the grandest failure because he had a vast courage . . . in that he attempted what he knew he probably couldn't do" (Inge 79). When pushed to place himself on this scale of "grandest failure," Faulkner would rank himself second because he knew that like Wolfe he too had attempted the impossible and was nearly electrocuted by divine fire. Like all geniuses, he imagined and envisioned greater than he could achieve, at least by his own lights. In a more honest moment of self-reflection, however, Faulkner ran his finger along a shelf of his own books and remarked, "Not a bad monument for a man to leave behind him" (Inge 98).

In 1930 Faulkner published a short story, "A Rose for Emily," in a nationally distributed magazine, *The Forum.* The editors had asked him to provide a biographical note to appear with the story, so with characteristic humor and exaggeration, he submitted the following: "Born male and single at early age in Mississippi. Quit school after five years in seventh grade. Got job in Grandfather's bank and learned medicinal value of his liquor. Grandfather thought janitor did it. Hard on janitor. War came. Liked British uniform. Got commission R. F. C., pilot. Crashed. Cost British gov't 2000 pounds. Was still pilot. Crashed. Cost British gov't 2000 pounds. King said, 'Well done.' Returned to Mississippi. Family got job: postmaster. Resigned by mutual agreement on part of two inspectors; accused of throwing all incoming mail into garbage can. How disposed of outgoing mail never proved. Inspectors foiled. Had $700. Went to Europe. Met

A ROSE for Emily

Drawings by Weldon Bailey

by WILLIAM FAULKNER

I

When Miss Emily Grierson died, our whole town went to her funeral: the men through a sort of respectful affection for a fallen monument, the women mostly out of curiosity to see the inside of her house, which no one save an old Negro manservant — a combined gardener and cook — had seen in at least ten years.

It was a big, squarish, frame house that had once been white, decorated with cupolas and spires and scrolled balconies in the heavily lightsome style of the seventies, set on what had once been our most select street. But garages and cotton gins had encroached and obliterated even the august names of that neighborhood; only Miss Emily's house was left, lifting its stubborn and coquettish decay

above the cotton wagons and the gasoline pumps — an eyesore among eyesores. And now Miss Emily had gone to join the representatives of those august names where they lay in the cedar-bemused cemetery among the ranked and anonymous graves of Union and Confederate soldiers who fell at the battle of Jefferson.

Alive, Miss Emily had been a tradition, a duty, and a care; a sort of hereditary obligation upon the town, dating from that day in 1894 when Colonel Sartoris, the mayor — he who fathered the edict that no Negro woman should appear on the streets without an apron — remitted her taxes, the dispensation dating from the death of her father on into perpetuity. Not that Miss Emily would have accepted charity.

APRIL 1930 233

el Sartoris invented an involved tale to fect that Miss Emily's father had loaned r to the town, which the town, as a matbusiness, preferred this way of repaying. a man of Colonel Sartoris' generation and ht could have invented it, and only a n could have believed it.

en the next generation, with its more n ideas, became mayors and aldermen, arrangement created some little dissatisn. On the first of the year they mailed tax notice. February came, and there o reply. They wrote her a formal letter, g her to call at the sheriff's office at her nience. A week later the mayor wrote mself, offering to call or to send his car r, and received in reply a note on paper of haic shape, in a thin, flowing calligraphy led ink, to the effect that she no longer out at all. The tax notice was also en-, without comment.

ey called a special meeting of the Board dermen. A deputation waited upon her, ed at the door through which no visitor passed since she ceased giving chinaing lessons eight or ten years earlier. They admitted by the old Negro into a dim hall which a stairway mounted into still more w. It smelled of dust and disuse — a close, smell. The Negro led them he parlor. It was furnished avy, leather-covered furni-When the Negro opened the s of one window, they could aat the leather was cracked; when they sat down, a faint rose sluggishly about their s, spinning with slow motes single sun-ray. On a tard gilt easel before the firestood a crayon portrait of Emily's father.

ey rose when she entered — a small, fat an in black, with a thin gold chain descendo her waist and vanishing into her belt, ag on an ebony cane with a tarnished gold Her skeleton was small and spare; perthat was why what would have been ly plumpness in another was obesity in She looked bloated, like a body long subed in motionless water, and of that pallid Her eyes, lost in the fatty ridges of her looked like two small pieces of coal pressed

into a lump of dough face to another while errand.

She did not ask th in the door and listened quietly until the spokesman came to a stumbling halt. Then they could hear the invisible watch ticking at the end of the gold chain.

Her voice was dry and cold. "I have no taxes in Jefferson. Colonel Sartoris explained it to me. Perhaps one of you can gain access to the city records and satisfy yourselves."

"But we have. We are the city authorities, Miss Emily. Didn't you get a notice from the sheriff, signed by him?"

"I received a paper, yes," Miss Emily said. "Perhaps he considers himself the sheriff. . . . I have no taxes in Jefferson."

"But there is nothing on the books to show that, you see. We must go by the —"

"See Colonel Sartoris. I have no taxes in Jefferson."

"But, Miss Emily— "

"See Colonel Sartoris. (Colonel Sartoris had been dead almost ten years.) "I have no taxes in Jefferson. Tobe!" The Negro appeared. "Show these gentlemen out."

II

So she vanquished them, horse and foot, just as she had vanquished their fathers thirty years before about the smell. That was two years after her father's death and a short time after her sweetheart — the one we believed would marry her — had deserted her. After her father's death she went out very little; after her sweetheart went away, people hardly saw her at all. A few of the ladies had the temerity to call, but were not received, and the only sign of life about the place was the Negro man — a young man then — going in and out with a market basket.

"Just as if a man — any man — could keep a kitchen properly," the ladies said; so they were not surprised when the smell developed. It was another link between the gross, teeming world and the high and mighty Griersons.

A neighbor, a woman, complained to the mayor, Judge Stevens, eighty years old.

Illustrations by Weldon Bailey for "A Rose for Emily," Faulkner's first published short story, which appeared in the April, 1930 issue of The Forum *magazine* man named Sherwood Anderson. Said, 'Why not write novels? Maybe won't have to work.' Did. *Soldiers' Pay*. Did. *Mosquitoes*. Did. *Sound and Fury*. Did. *Sanctuary*, out next year. Now flying again. Age 32. Own and operate own typewriter" (*Letters* 47). Except for stretching the truth in behalf of comedy, the facts are not too far wrong as a thumbnail overview of his life and career up to 1930.

He was born into a family of lawyers, soldiers, politicians, and businessmen. Faulkner's great-grandfather, William Clark Falkner (1825-1889), had been a prominent Mississippi plantation owner, Civil War officer, post-war railroad builder, and author of a best-selling romance called *The White Rose of Memphis* (1881). He was one of the first to change the spelling of the family name away from the original "Faulkner." So colorful and full of intrigues and romantic gestures was his life that it

The typewriter and desk used by Faulkner to compose his novels

read like a piece of fiction itself and formed the substance of family myth and folklore. His great-grandson would inevitably draw on it for his own creative writing, using him as the prototype for Colonel John Sartoris, who, along with his descendants, would figure in several major novels.

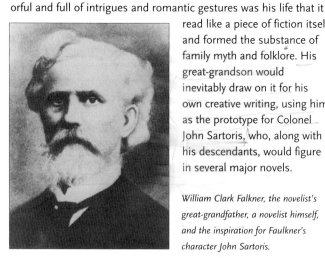

William Clark Falkner, the novelist's great-grandfather, a novelist himself, and the inspiration for Faulkner's character John Sartoris.

The Colonel, as he was called, fought in the Mexican war, raised two military units to fight in the Civil War, carried on guerilla warfare against Federal troops, built a railroad after the war, and was elected to the Mississippi legislature. On the same day he was elected, he was shot down in the street by a bitter rival. No stranger to brawling and violence, he was himself responsible for killing two men in separate arguments.

It has only recently been discovered that in all likelihood Colonel Falkner fathered one or more children with one of his black slaves and initiated a black Falkner family that would co-exist with his own. Whether or not William Faulkner knew about this relationship is not clear, but it is true that the theme of mixed blood or miscegenation plays a prominent part in his fiction; in fact, the literary character based on the Colonel, John Sartoris, has such a relationship, so it must have crossed his mind. From Thomas Jefferson on, historic evidence now suggests that many prominent Southern men crossed the sexual color line and left behind black descendants.

Faulkner's grandfather, John Wesley Thompson Falkner (1848-1922), called the "Young Colonel" because of his father and not any military experience of his own, was a lawyer, banker, and politician. A heavy drinker and irascible in his old age, he served as a model for Bayard Sartoris in his grandson's fiction. His oldest son and Faulkner's father was Murry Cuthbert Falkner (1870-1932), who brought the family tradition of public success to an end but maintained the private dissipation.

John Wesley Thompson Falkner and wife, Sallie Murry, the novelist's paternal grandparents.

Murry Cuthbert Falkner, the novelist's father.

Right, Falkner's mother Maud Butler Falkner, in 1896, about the time of her marriage.

The Falkner family penchant for violence was visited upon him when a rival shot him in the mouth but failed to kill him. His only interest was the railroad. He settled in, Oxford, Mississippi, in 1902 to raise his family, and after several business failures, he became business manager and secretary at the University of Mississippi in Oxford. His lack of ambition and self-confidence earned him a low opinion in the eyes of his sons, especially the eldest.

The first-born was William Cuthbert Falkner. Born on September 25, 1897, in New Albany, before the family moved to Ripley, and then Oxford in 1902, he grew up in a household full not only of family myth and legend but the presence of several dynamic and dominating personalities. One was Sallie Murry Falkner (1850-1906), his paternal grandmother, an independent and strong-willed woman who usually got her own way with grandchildren, church, and com-

Maud Butler Falkner holding her infant son William.

Above, childhood photograph of Faulkner at about age one.
Right, early photograph of William Faulkner.

munity alike. (When the United Daughters of the Confederacy refused to do what she wished with a proposed statue of a Confederate soldier, she resigned and started her own initiative.) Another was Lelia Dean Swift Butler (1849-1907), his maternal grandmother, an accomplished painter in her own right who taught young Billy how to draw. Though pious and stern, he fondly called her "Damuddy," the same nickname used by the Compson children for their grandmother in *The Sound and The Fury*.

His mother, Maud Butler Falkner (1871-1960), equally iron-willed, was an intelligent and educated woman who read books and assumed the major responsibility for seeing to her children's educational and emotional needs. Her motto, posted on a sign in the kitchen, was "DON'T COMPLAIN—DON'T EXPLAIN." Probably young Billy was her favorite, and she would encourage and defend him all his life. She was of immeasurable influence on his success. A final influential presence in the household was Caroline Barr (c. 1840-1940), known as "Mammy" Cally," a former slave who joined the family to help raise the children and whose attention to Billy earned her his undying devotion. He called her his "second mother." Little wonder with such strong and powerful role models, Faulkner's fiction would largely be populated by dominating and independent female characters, black and white, who stand up and cast a strong shadow.

Faulkner had three brothers. Murry Charles Falkner, Jr. (1899-1975), or Jack, served in the military in both World Wars, became a lawyer and a pilot, and spent most of his career as an agent for the FBI. John Wesley Thompson Falkner (1901-1963), or Johncy, studied engineering, worked as a pilot and a farmer, and finally decided to pursue a literary career like his brother. His several novels, as well as his paintings, brought him a modest degree of success. The youngest, Dean Swift Falkner (1907-1935), was an impetuous and restless young man who was tragically killed in a plane crash at an air show. Because Faulkner loaned him the money for flying lessons, he always felt responsible for his death, and he raised his daughter as if she were his own. (Except for Murry, most of the rest of the family would adopt Faulkner's restored spelling of the family name.)

Despite the house full of interesting and assertive personalities, Faulkner had a typical Southern nineteenth-century childhood, which featured large families, spacious houses, full yards to play in, and ample food and clothing. There was sufficient family success and position in the background to make the Falkners feel a notch above the common folk who populated

Childhood portrait of the Faulk brothers, Jack, John, and Willia

the community, not quite aristocrats but something akin to it. A degree of snobbishness and self-importance entered their relationships with others, but young Billy, with his small stature and high voice, often felt alienation and shyness rather than superiority in his games with other children. But one little girl, Lida Estelle Oldham, whose family had moved to Oxford when she was only seven, paid attention to him, and they would become a good deal more than fast friends. Rumor has it that she fell in love with him on first sight and decided she would marry him, but later when they courted, her family disapproved and forced her to marry a better prospect.

Left, Estelle Oldham in 191 the inspiration for and rec of Faulkner's early love po

Below, Mammy Callie (Caroline Barr) who helpe raise Faulkner

While Billy was a good student when he applied himself, he soon became restive and bored with formal education. He learned a good deal more outside of class in the volumes of fiction and poetry his mother shared with him: Shakespeare, Fielding, Balzac, Hugo, Melville, Mark Twain, Conrad, and Joel Chandler Harris among them. But he especially learned from his immediate milieu in terms of conversation, stories, and real-life events. He gloried in the romantic tales about his great-grandfather and listened to the stories about events in the Civil War recounted by his grandfather and Civil War veterans. He heard from Mammy Callie about life among slaves on the plantation, and listened to the gory details of local tragedies—murders, lynchings, and duels over women. He went on train rides, automobile excursions, and unsuccessfully tried to build an airplane based on plans in a boys' magazine. Billy's childhood world was a place for the imagination to thrive, and he would remember it all and transpose it into pure literary gold in his fiction to come.

He began to tell stories himself and could charm others into doing his tasks in exchange for a story. As a niece once reported, "It got so that when Billy told you something, you never knew if it was the truth or just something he had made up" (Blotner 35). When asked by a teacher what he wanted to be when he grew up, Billy said, "I want to be a writer like my great-granddaddy" (Blotner 23). Faulkner had found his life's work by the time he was nine years old.

Rather than study, he spent his days working in his father's livery stable, pitching hay, playing high school football and baseball, learning to be a Boy Scout, and hunting. These experiences too would feed into the storehouse of his imagination only to emerge in his fiction, especially the several bear hunts into the woods. When he was nineteen, his father got him a job as a bookkeeper in the First National Bank of Oxford, which his grandfather had helped establish and served as its first president. Faulkner claimed he would steal drinks from his grandfather's liquor supply in his desk. None of these occupations lasted very long as the young Faulkner spent most of his time drawing cartoons and writing stories and poems. He shared these not only with his friend Estelle, to whom he paid increasing attention, but with a young Oxford law student named Phil Stone, a graduate of Yale University and a man of cultivated literary taste.

Stone supplemented the reading Faulkner had done with his mother with a series of books by modern and contemporary writers such as Sherwood Anderson, Conrad Aiken,

A young Phil Stone in 1918, who would guide Faulkner's early readings in modernism and help him into print.

Left, Gathright-Reed Drug Co. off Oxford Square. The owner, W. M. "Mac" Reed, helped Faulkner wrap and mail his manuscripts to New York and loaned him books out of his paperback lending library.

Below, the courthouse in Oxford Square was built in 1871 after the previous court house had been destroyed by Federal troops during the Civil War.

F. Scott Fitzgerald, Aldous Huxley, D. H. Lawrence, Willa Cather, W. B. Yeats, and the poets found in such little magazines as *Poetry* and *The Dial*. Through Stone, he was introduced to fellow Oxford townsman and nascent writer Stark Young. Stone served not only to educate Faulkner in the latest trends in contemporary writing but to stoke the fires of his ambition by encouraging his earliest serious literary efforts.

In the spring of 1918 he joined Stone at Yale, where Stone was completing a law degree, and earned his keep by working as a clerk at the Winchester Repeating Arms Co. under the last name now spelled "Faulkner." As both young men were of age, they naturally were inclined to join thousands of others who were signing up in

Left, illustration by Faulkner for the university student annual
Ole Miss, 1916-1917.

Below, Requisition for payment by the University of Mississippi
of five dollars to W. C. Handy's Jazz Band for their performance at a Friday night dance in 1918.

University of Mississippi

(Requisition for purchase of supplies or articles needed for use of the University or for work to be done on
University property, to be made out by Professors or other officers concerned.)

UNIVERSITY, MISS.,.....4/1......191 8

To the Secretary:

Request is hereby made for the purchase of articles listed hereon, for the performance of the work indicated.
The articles named are for the use of the University and the work named is necessary for the proper preservation
and use of University property.

The articles needed are specified in detail, and will probably cost $....5.00..................
to be paid out of funds available for....Picture Show.....................
Respectfully submitted.

Received.................191....
Ordered.................191....   Prof. of.....................

LIST: *Due W. C. Handy   for 'Handy's
Band. Music for Friday Nigs.*

$5.00

Cpt. Confeyfield

Illustration by Faulkner for Ole Miss, 1920-1921. W. C. Handy frequently brought his
jazz band from memphis to play at university social events. Faulkner borrowed the title
of his short story, "That Evening Sun," from the first line of Handy's "St. Louis Blues."

Cartoon by Faulkner for Ole Miss, 1919-1920.

Le grand   Americaine- Parlez-vous Anglais, mam'zelle?
La petite Francaise — Mais oui, m'sieur, un peu; Do you love me! heez me queek! Damn! 'ell!

SOCIAL ACTIVITIES

Organizations

Illustrations by Faulkner for Ole Miss, 1919-1920.

RED & BLUE

CLASSES

A.E.F. CLUB

THINK HOW MANY TIMES THIS BIRD'S
BEEN KISSED. HE GOT A CROIX
DE GUERRE, WITH PALMS.

FISH, FLESH, FOWL

Illustrations by Faulkner for Ole Miss, *1920-1921.*

the military with the Allies in World War I. Like Hemingway, Fitzgerald, John Dos Passos, and E. E. Cummings, Faulkner too wanted to experience the thrill and danger of first-hand combat and enter the crucible that proved courage and manhood, a romantic myth that would bring instead disillusionment and despair to those who actually experienced it.

Although the facts of the matter are vague, apparently Faulkner was rejected by the Aviation Branch of the United States Army's Signal Corps, so he determined to join the Canadian Royal Air Force. To do so, he passed himself off as English, with faked accent, place of birth, and letters of reference from a fictional British clergyman. From this time on, he would maintain the new spelling of the family name. He entered training at a camp near Toronto, but after 179 days of schooling, the war was concluded before Faulkner earned his stripes. How much flying he actually experienced remains unknown, but he returned home to Oxford resplendent in an officer's uniform, wearing the pipes of a lieutenant, and carrying a swagger stick, with lots of stories about combat experience in the air and war wounds, as well as comic tales about crashing planes during training— twice. This was

Taylor Groce and Restaur in nearby Taylor, Mississippi, where Oxfore residents still to eat catfish

the first of several roles he would play in the eyes of others as his life and career would lead him into public scrutiny.

When not striking a pose in or out of uniform around town, which earned him the nickname of "Count," and not drinking with friends in brothels and gambling houses in Memphis, New Orleans, and other towns, Faulkner continued to work on his poetry. The romantic focus of his work was gone, however, since Estelle had married while he was in Canada and moved with her lawyer husband, Cornell Franklin, to Hawaii. Whenever she returned for a visit, he would spend time with her and show her his writing. The poetry was both pastoral and modern, combining the influences of his early loves, Algernon Swinbume and A. E. Housman, with the more recent work of T. S. Eliot and Ezra Pound. While competent and full of aesthetic promise, it was not highly original, although one poem, "L'Apres-Midi d'un Faune," was accepted by the prestigious *New Republic* and published in its issue of August 6, 1919. The appearance of his first poem in print was followed by his first short story, "Landing in Luck," based on his military experience, in November in the campus newspaper, *The Mississippian.*

Faulkner registered as a special student in September of 1919 and signed up for courses in French, Spanish, and Shakespeare. He was a disinterested student, although he would eventually gain a decent command of French, a language and culture he greatly admired. Because other family members had been involved, he was pledged and initiated into the social fraternity Sigma Alpha Epsilon. At semester's end, even though he reportedly refused to take the final examinations, he earned an A in French, a B in Spanish, and a D in English.

He produced hand-lettered and illustrated collections of poems, including an experimental verse play called *Marionettes,* as well as an 88-page bound typescript of a poetry sequence, *Vision in Spring,* presented to Estelle on one of her visits home in the summer of 1921. Though derivative and imperfect in design, the eighteen poems reflect a concern with persona and perspective that would carry over into his mature fiction. His time spent on such romantic and fruitless endeavors, and his occasionally careless dress, soon turned his earlier name into "Count No 'Count'" among those who never knew how to take his affectations and aloof attitude, which concealed his personal unhappiness and creative frustrations.

Some relief was offered by an invitation from Stark Young, just beginning to find his way as a critic, to visit him in New York and try the literary waters of that city. To support himself Faulkner took a job as a clerk in the Lord & Taylor Doubleday Bookstore arranged by Young through his friend who managed the store, Elizabeth Prall, later Mrs. Sherwood Anderson. Finding no entry into the literary life of the publishing center of the United States, by December of 1921 Faulkner returned home to accept an appointment arranged for him by Phil Stone as postmaster of the university post office at a salary of $1,500 a year, his first decent paying and regular job.

Remarkably, the position would last almost three years, despite the cavalier attitude with which he treated the responsibilities. Mail was not promptly posted or forwarded, customers were neglected, and magazines were held until he had a chance to read them. As a result, Faulkner was exposed to some of the best contemporary literature and criticism contained in The American Mercury, The Nation, The New

Carbon copy of a letter from Chancellor of the University of Mississippi to Faulkner about his conduct as campus postmaster.

September 27, 1922

Mr. W. C. Falkner, Postmaster,
University, Mississippi.

Dear Mr. Falkner:

This is to acknowledge receipt of your communication relative to inviting constructive criticism of the University Postoffice. So far as this office is concerned, I have little of which to complain. The few minor irregularities which we may have noticed were possibly due to no fault of yours.

I should tell you, however, that several persons have complained to me about the delay in receiving their mail, stating that letters from Jackson and other nearby places arrive several days later than they should.

With the large number of students now on the campus, it behooves you to be careful and accurate in making up and distributing mail, and you should have all the assistance necessary to render the most efficient service. I appreciate the expressions contained in your letter, and I hope no further complaint of any irregularity in the mail service will reach this office.

Very truly yours,

JNP:RMC

Chancellor

This satiric advertisement was a hoax that circulated on the campus of the University of Mississippi in 1924 while Faulkner was serving as campus postmaster.

Republic, North American Review, The Dial, and The Little Review, as well as other quarterlies and little magazines on their way to the university library. Complaints eventually brought an investigation and an official reprimand from the postal authorities, in the wake of which he resigned in October of 1924. While accounts of his comment vary, Faulkner has been quoted as saying, "I reckon I'll be at the beck and call of folks with money all my life, but thank God I won't ever again have to be at the beck and call of every son of a bitch who's got two cents to buy a stamp" (Blotner 118).

One reason he probably felt confident enough to walk away from a regular salary was the fact that his first book was on press. His friend Phil Stone had stepped in to help jumpstart his career by agreeing to subsidize its publication. The manuscript was a cycle of poems he had completed the previous year called *The Marble Faun,* and the Four Seas Company of Boston agreed to issue an edition of one thousand copies for $400. The nineteen pastoral eclogues that constitute *The Marble Faun* are spoken by a marble statue of a faun and are arranged according to the season. Like most of Faulkner's early poetry, these dwell on the traditional themes of loss, change, deception, and frustrated desire, and the heavy influence of John Keats is evident. It was barely reviewed but at least one critic, John McClure of the New Orleans *Double Dealer* (January 25, 1925), found it full of promise and ability and a sign of a major talent on the horizon. But it did not sell well and made no headway in the world of letters.

By the time *The Marble Faun* was published on December 15, 1924, Faulkner had left for New Orleans with plans to visit his former boss, Elizabeth Prall, and meet her new husband, Sherwood Anderson. Originally he had intended to earn his passage on a boat to Europe, but that plan failed and he had to find a living once more. He barely scraped by on his earnings by contributing essays, sketches, stories, and poems to *The Double Dealer* magazine and the *Times-Picayune* newspaper, pieces that were five-finger exercises in developing a sense of style. Less likely were the stories he later told of running moonshine liquor for the local bootleggers or flying with an air circus passing through town (although he may have gone up with one of the pilots a few times).

New Orleans was a lively gathering place for a host of young artists, writers, and intellectuals gathered around two centers of attention—Anderson, then the most influential and respected figure on the American literary scene, and the editorial offices of *The Double Dealer,* which was publishing all the best young writers. Faulkner found himself immersed in a rich milieu of aesthetic conversation, dominated by the influences of Sigmund Freud, Sir James Frazer, and James Joyce. Phil Stone had given him a copy of Joyce's *Ulysses* the year before, which he obviously read, although he would later deny having done so. While he mainly listened and remained on the edges of the discussion groups, Faulkner and Anderson became good friends and

Faulkner in New Orleans, 1925.

spent time together concocting tall tales about a descendant of Andrew Jackson who raised sheep in the swamp and turned from a half-horse and half-alligator into a half-man, half-sheep, and finally a half-shark. Anderson once warned him, "You've got too much talent. You can do it too easy, in too many different ways. If you're not careful, you'll never write anything" (*Essays* 7).

Inspired by Anderson's example and thriving in the glow of the older writer's words of praise and encouragement, Faulkner began work on a novel. Working at a steady pace, he quickly completed the manuscript which he called "Mayday" and which Anderson recommended to his publisher, Boni & Liveright of New York. One story Faulkner later told was that Anderson had agreed to recommend it if he didn't have to read the manuscript, but this may have been a reflection of the falling out he had with Anderson later. Faulkner had written an essay for the Dallas *Morning News* in which he faulted his mentor for his midwestern provincialism, lack of humor, and limited artistic growth since his first and best works. He would also satirize his style in a small volume called *Sherwood Anderson & Other Famous Creoles,* illustrated by Faulkner's roommate and artist William Spratling. The senior author was neither understanding nor forgiving.

In the company of Spratling, Faulkner finally embarked on a freighter ship out of New Orleans on July 7, 1925. Arriving in

WS 1925

Genoa, they passed through Italy and Switzerland to arrive in Paris. There they settled into an inexpensive hotel on the Left Bank and frequented the Louvre and other galleries to study the paintings of Cezanne, Degas, Matisse, Picasso, and other moderns. Faulkner wrote to his mother, "don't faint—I am growing a beard" (*Letters* 12), and he later sent a small sketch of himself with the new growth and a face that appears to be a cross between Mephistopheles and

*Portrait o
Faulkner b
William
Spratling, wh
shared a roor
with him i
New Orlear
and travele
wih him t
Europe in 192*

a faun. He frequented the sidewalk cafés but had few contacts with the expatriate writers inhabiting Paris, going only so far as to view Joyce from a distance. He later reported, "I knew of Joyce, and I would go to some effort to go to the cafe that he inhabited to look at him. But that was the only literary man that I remember seeing in Europe in those days" (*University* 58). More importantly, he was constantly writing— letters to his mother, notebook entries, articles, poems, as well as two novels, one of which would become his second published novel.

Using his time to maximum effect, Faulkner saw more of France by train and by foot and visited the major battlefields of World War I in which he had longed to participate as a flying ace in dogfights with German aviators. So strong was that desire that he later invented the tale that he had been shot down over Paris and bore a metal plate in his head as a result of the wounds. He briefly visited England, but the high costs of things drove him back to Paris. By December he was ready to return home and took passage on a ship. He and Spratling left on December 10, and after a visit to Oxford, Faulkner settled into an apartment in New Orleans with him and continued his writing.

While Faulkner was traveling in Europe, "Mayday" had been accepted for publication and would appear under the title *Soldiers' Pay* on February 25, 1926, in a printing of 2,500 copies, most of which sold within three months. This story of a returned Southern veteran of

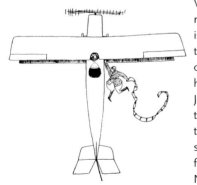

World War I is a somber and mannered combination of realism, psychology, social observation, and myth that fits the mold of modernism. Hints of T. S. Eliot haunt the characters, and the Joycean use of myth is subjected to witty parody. Most reviewers tended to see it as an ineffective synthesis of the current fads in fiction, but John McClure in the New Orleans *Times-Picayune*

Illustration b[y] Faulkner for university stu[dent] humor maga[zine] The Scream, 1925.

(April 11, 1926) once again weighed in with warm praise and described it as the most noteworthy first novel to appear that year. In the Nashville *Tennessean* (April 11, 1926), where he edited a popular book page, Fugitive poet Donald Davidson found it a powerful and artistically pleasing performance and superior, in fact, to the much praised 1921 novel of World War I by John Dos Passos, *Three Soldiers*. On the home front, the response was not entirely happy. Because of the sexual content, his father refused to read the novel, and one relative suggested that he ought to stay out of town. Phil Stone offered a complimentary copy to the university library, but they refused to accept it.

Since Estelle, his dream girl, was married and living in Hawaii, Faulkner tried to put her out of mind and centered his attention on an attractive and unconventional young woman named Helen Baird, who aspired to be a sculptor. He had met her through friends in New Orleans, and her blunt honesty, creativity, and spontaneity strongly appealed to him. They swam and spent time together, and soon Faulkner was writing specifically for her. He presented her with a hand-lettered illuminated volume containing an allegorical tale about a young knight in pursuit of the woman he loves, only to discover finally that she is Death. Called *Mayday,* the rejected title of his first novel, it existed in an edition of one copy. In a similar hand-written and hand-drawn fashion, he assembled another volume called *Helen: A Courtship,* a sixteen-poem cycle devoted to his ideal conception of a woman as based on Helen Baird. Faulkner had fallen in love, and this was intended as his proposal of marriage. She was fond of him but unimpressed by his creative efforts, so she rejected him. She would reappear as a character in his fiction, and he dedicated his second novel to her, although by the time it appeared, she was already married to another man.

He had started writing *Mosquitoes* while be was in Paris and completed it after his return to the states by September of 1926. It was a smug *roman à clef* based directly on his acquaintances and experiences in New Orleans but inspired more by the satiric authors of the Jazz Age who crowded the literary marketplace. Fitzgerald's *The Great Gatsby* appeared in 1925, and in England Aldous Huxley was publishing his popular series of cynical social novels. Faulkner had read the first of the Huxley series, *Chrome Yellow,* in 1921, and it bears striking similarities with *Mosquitoes.* Boni & Liveright published it on April 30, 1927.

If *Soldiers' Pay* had been perceived as too much of its own time, this was especially true of *Mosquitoes.* John McClure, usually the first with praise, in the *Times-Picayune* seemed to have grown disenchanted with the sarcasm, cruelty, and eroticism he saw in the book, or perhaps he was simply being defensive because so many of his friends show up in the novel (including even a self-portrait of Faulkner). Lillian Hellman, writing for the New York *Herald Tribune,* despite spotting evident influences of Joyce and Huxley, thought the

novel clever, versatile, brilliant, and "full of the fine kind of swift and lusty writing that comes from a healthy, fresh pen" (June 19, 1927). Davidson maintained his support in the Nashville *Tennessean,* noting that "Faulkner sits in the seat of the scornful with a manner somewhat reminiscent of James Joyce, but with such gracious ease that you almost overlook the savagery" (July 3, 1927). The other reviewers were mixed in their responses, but nearly all found something to admire in Faulkner's emerging competence as a novelist.

Jacket of Faulkner's se published no Mosquitoes.

Faulkner's breach with Anderson and his disenchantment with Helen did not help maintain the charm of New Orleans, so he returned to Oxford for Christmas of 1926. There was another attraction too. Estelle had just returned home to begin divorce proceedings against her husband; both of them were unable to remain faithful in their marriage. Charmed by her eight-year-old daughter, Victoria, Faulkner presented the child with a hardbound typed story called *The Wishing Tree,* which demonstrated no small talent in writing fiction for children, although he would never repeat the effort. It was published posthumously in 1967. His major creative projects were manuscripts for a novel to be called "Father Abraham," about an avaricious redneck family called the Snopes, characters to which he would return in later stories and novels, although this one would remain unpublished, and another called "Flags in the Dust," a major work in the canon as things turned out.

In both manuscripts, Faulkner had begun to draw on local Mississippi history and the experiences of his own family. Anderson had already cautioned him in the days of their close friendship and walks together that the best writing comes out of what one knows best, that is one's

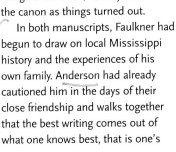

own native locale and region: "You're a country boy; all you know is that little patch up there in Mississippi where you started from. But that's all right too. It's America too . . ." (*Essays* 8). Halfway through writing his third novel, Faulkner later said, "suddenly I discovered that writing was a mighty fine thing—you could make people stand up on their own hind legs and cast a shadow. I felt I had all these people, and as soon as I discovered it I wanted to bring them all back" (Inge 35). By the time he finished the writing, he concluded, "I discovered that my own little postage stamp of native soil was worth writing about and that I would never live long enough to exhaust it, and that by sublimating the actual to the apocryphal I would have complete liberty to use whatever talent I might have to its absolute top" (Meriwether 255). Appropriately enough, when the novel appeared, it would be dedicated "To Sherwood Anderson, through whose kindness I was first published, with the belief that this book will give him no reason to regret that fact."

But the way to the press for the third novel had not been easy. The manuscript began as a short story about an old man meditating on his family's past and its tendency toward violence and lost causes, but it soon expanded into a complex narrative about a family called Sartoris, especially the twin brothers John and Bayard. John was killed in an air battle during World War I and Bayard feels responsible for his death. On his return home he engages in reckless behavior and is unable to settle down to a conventional life. He wrecks an automobile with his grandfather in the car, and this gives the old Colonel a fatal heart attack. Bayard finally disappears and dies testing an experimental aircraft. He leaves behind a grieving aunt, Jenny DuPre, who has witnessed the deaths of several male family members over fruitless causes, and a pregnant widow, Narcissa Benbow, whose brother Horace has harbored incestuous feelings for her.

This story of two generations of a Southern version of landed aristocracy is set in a fully developed community of people who populate what Faulkner called Yoknapatawpha County, a name borrowed from an actual river and which he said meant in Chickasaw language "water runs slow through flat land" but with

Caricature of Faulkner's fictional Yoknapatawpha County by Campbell Grant.

no supporting authority. The word, according to Faulkner, was to be pronounced "YOCK-na-pa-TAWpha" *(University* 74). What became evident was that Yoknapatawpha was based on the actual Lafayette County in Mississippi, the fictional town of Jefferson was based on Oxford, and the Sartoris family reflected his own family history. As he said, he liked all the characters so much that he wanted to bring them back, and he did in some nine novels and numerous short stories to come. So real did the fictional community become that he could later map it out in some detail—an area of 2,400 square miles and a population of 6,298 whites and 9,313 blacks—with the legend, "William Faulkner, sole owner and proprietor."

The length and complexity of the plot of *Flags in the Dust* became unwieldy as it began to involve not only the Sartorises and the Benbows but the bank bookkeeper Byron Snopes, who writes obscene letters to Narcissa Benbow; the sewing-machine salesman V. K. Suratt (later changed to Ratliff); Belle Mitchell, who is courted by Horace Benbow; and numerous others. He sent it off to the publisher in mid-October of 1927 with the note, "I have written THE book. . . . I believe it is the damdest book you'll look at this year, and any other publisher" *(Letters* 38). By mid-November Horace Liveright wrote back that the manuscript was neither publishable nor salvageable: "It is diffuse and non-integral with neither very much plot development nor character development. . . . The story really doesn't get anywhere and has a thousand loose ends" (Blotner 205).

Deeply disappointed, Faulkner sent it off to other publishers, eleven of whom rejected it before Harcourt Brace and Company

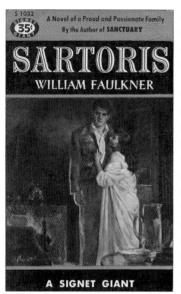

Cover of pa
back edition
Sartoris, 19
which Faulk
wanted to c
"Flags in the
Dust." This
the first nov
deal with th
fictional wor
Yoknapataw
County.

agreed to take it but with substantial revision and reduction. Unable to face it alone, he called on an old friend, writer Ben Wasson, then working in New York as a literary agent, to help him. Together they reduced the manuscript by a quarter and sharpened the focus. The abbreviated version was published not as "Flags in the Dust," Faulkner's title, but as *Sartoris* on January 31, 1929. Most of the critics, the old faithful as well as the skeptical, felt that Faulkner had come into his own. Henry Nash Smith, in the Dallas *Morning News* (February 17, 1929), greeted the novel as the product of "one of the most promising talents for fiction in contemporary America." Davidson, in the *Tennessean* (April 14, 1929), stated that "as a stylist and as an acute observer of human nature, I think Mr. Faulkner is the equal of any except three or four American novelists who stand at the very top." Anticipating the mythological and allegorical theories that critics would apply to Faulkner later, Davidson noted, "I cannot help suspecting some allegorical meaning is in *Sartoris.*"

While *Sartoris* was experiencing its birth throes, Faulkner was involved in planting the seeds and nurturing what would be his greatest effort and masterwork. In early 1928 he started writing a short story called "Twilight," an earlier version of which he may have written in Paris in 1925, about a little girl and her brothers who are sent away from the house after the death of their grandmother because they are too young to understand the removal of the body and the funeral preparations. "So I, who never had a sister," he recalled, "set out to make myself a beautiful and tragic little girl" *(Essays* 300). Once she appeared on the page and was named Candace Compson, or Caddie, he decided "I loved her so much I couldn't decide to give her life just for the duration of one short story. She deserved more than that. So my novel was created, almost in spite of myself' (Coindreau 41).

According to Faulkner, who was called on to speak about the novel's origin on numerous occasions, the manuscript grew incrementally in the light of several images and narrative decisions. One image had to do with Caddie getting dirty by splashing in a brook and falling in, with the smallest brother crying over the event until she would stop playing to comfort him. Another was of Caddie climbing a pear tree to peek into the house at the funeral and her three brothers looking up at her exposed muddy drawers. He would always claim that image was "the only thing in literature that would ever move me very much . . ." *(Essays* 299).

He felt that the traditional third-person narrative somehow was not up to the task of telling her story. The use of point of view or narrative voice was always a major technical interest of Faulkner's, and he would experiment with how a story is told throughout his fiction. So he said, "I decided that the most effective way to tell that [story] would be through the eyes of the idiot child [Benjy Compson], who didn't even know, couldn't understand what was going on. And this went for a while, and I thought it was going to be a ten-page story. The first thing I knew I had about a hundred pages. I finished, and I still hadn't told that story. So I chose

t. Hamilton Hill, which have served to inspire the mpson home The Sound nd the Fury.

another one of the children [Quentin Compson], let him try. That went for a hundred pages, and I still hadn't told that story. So I picked out the other one [Jason Compson], the one that was nearest to what we call sane to see if maybe he could unravel the thing. He talked for a hundred pages, he hadn't told it, then I let Faulkner try it for a hundred pages. And when I got done, it still wasn't finished, and so twenty years later I wrote an appendix, tried to tell that story. That's all I was doing on the first page, was trying to tell what to me seemed a beautiful and tragic story of that doomed little girl climbing the pear tree to see the funeral" (Inge 214). In other words, he tried to tell the same story from four different points of view but failed in his own eyes to capture the essence of his vision.

While this narrative structure is one of the most striking and innovative things about the book, aside from his use of stream-of-consciousness and floating movement back and forth in time, Faulkner's explanation only serves to simplify rather than clarify the nature of his accomplishment, which is a good deal more than the same story told in four different ways. The successive chapters do reflect on each other and elucidate the larger narrative, but each speaker provides an entirely different voice and a story almost independent of the others. Reading the novel is like finding oneself in a hall of mirrors. All the images seem to be of the same person but distortion and the lack of a central image lead the eye in twenty different directions at once. Having Benjy tell the story reminded Faulkner of the line from Shakespeare's *Macbeth,* "a tale, told by an idiot, full of sound and fury," but the remainder of the quotation does not apply—"signifying nothing."

What *The Sound and the Fury* does signify is the emotional collapse and moral failure of a Southern family that once occupied a major place in Mississippi society and claimed among its ancestors a Civil War brigadier general and a governor of the state. The father, Jason Compson III, has allowed his law practice to fail and is left to sit on his porch lost in dipsomania. His wife, Caroline Bascomb Compson, is a neurotic who complains constantly about everything and pretends infirmity while trying to maintain a façade

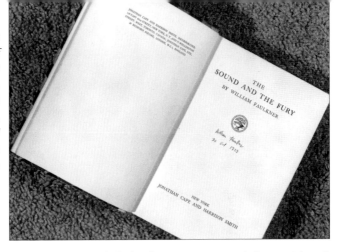

of gentility. Her alcoholic brother, Maury Bascomb, has no job and is supported by the family. Among the children, her second born, Jason IV, is her favorite because he is more like the Bascombs— cold, rational, and calculating.

The oldest son, Quentin, is trapped in his own emotional prison because he cannot square the sordid world around him with the virtues of honor and truth he has been taught to respect by the Code of the Old South. He is obsessed by an incestuous love for his younger sister, Caddie, and when she abandons herself to a passing lover, the loss of family honor and chastity drives him to morbid distraction and eventual suicide. A child born to Caddie as a result of the seduction is fatefully named after him. The youngest brother Benjy is born retarded, and he finds solace only in the smell and touch of Caddie. The family is held together by the strong and compelling presence of Dilsey Gibson, a black maid whose faith and serenity allow her to understand and respond to their needs at great sacrifice to herself. Only she has the clarity of vision to embrace the present in all its tragic circumstance and foresee the future: the death of Mrs. Compson, the institutionalization of Benjy, Caddie's disappearance (last seen on the arm of a German Nazi officer), and Jason's loss of his money to the young Quentin, who seems bent on repeating her mother's life of dissipation. Any summary such as this barely begins to do justice to the depth of the plot, the range of emotions, and the complexity of themes that characterize this profound and defiant novel.

Faulkner had finished the first draft of *The Sound and the Fury* by the end of September, since he carried the manuscript with him to New York in October when he went to work with Ben Wasson on revising *Sartoris*. His habit was to write out his fiction in longhand and then revise it in the process of typing it, so he labored on the typing of *The Sound and the Fury*, while Wasson did the lion's share of work on the revision of *Sartoris* to meet an October deadline. When he had finally finished the typescript, he threw it on the bed in Wasson's room and said, "Read this, Bud. It's a son-of-a-bitch" (Blotner 225). Writing his great aunt Bama, he told her that he had written "the damndest book I ever read. I don't believe anyone will publish it for ten years" *(Letters* 41). In retrospect he would claim, "When I finished *The Sound and the Fury* I discovered that there is actually something to which the shabby term Art not only can, but must, be applied. . . . With *The Sound and the Fury* I learned to read and quit reading, since I have read nothing since" *(Essays* 207). It was also his habit to go on a drinking spree after finishing a project, and he drank so heavily in this case that he was found unconscious in his room by friends a few days later.

Turned down as he knew it would be by both Liveright and Harcourt, *The Sound and the Fury* did impress an editor at Harcourt, Harrison Smith, who was about to begin his own publishing house. So it was accepted for publication by the Jonathan Cape and Harrison Smith firm. Faulkner headed home in December and started work on another novel only to be interrupted by a pleasant circumstance. Estelle's divorce had become final on April 29, 1929. Gathering together what funds he could in terms of advances from his publisher, he finally married the girl of his dreams on June 20. They went to Pascagoula, Mississippi, for their honeymoon, but it proved to be an unhappy beginning for their marriage. Somehow the strains of their frustrated lives apart crashed in on them, they drank too much, and Estelle tried to walk off into the water one evening. It may have been simply a

dramatic gesture of some sort, but it was a harbinger of things to come, as their lives together would be neither easy nor tranquil.

The Sound and the Fury was published on October 7, 1929. Predictably, some reviewers did not know what to make of the novel's experimental structure and innovative style, despite an appreciative pamphlet by novelist Evelyn Scott that came with the review copy. The more perceptive critics, and there were many, praised the work for raising the provincial to the level of the universal, for expanding the boundaries of the American novel, and restoring their faith in the art form and its emerging practitioners. Julia K. W. Baker, writing for the *Times-Picayune* (June 29, 1930), wrote that *"The Sound and the Fury* is one of the finest works in the tragic mode yet to appear in America. With it Mr. Faulkner is definitely established as one of the most gifted of contemporary novelists. He is the only American who seems capable of rivaling James Joyce. . . . It is highly original. You have not read anything like it." Whatever the nature or tenor of the reviewers' responses, from sarcasm to adulation, it was clear that a major talent had arrived on the American and world literary scene.

While he would be pleased with the response to *The Sound and the Fury,* he knew in advance that it would earn very little money. Thus five months before his marriage he had to forswear his oath to shut a door between himself and the literary marketplace and try to write something that would surely sell. He began writing what would become *Sanctuary,* a novel that would do just that but bring him notoriety as well. Drawing on popular fiction of the detective and murder mystery type, stories of gangsters and criminals in the newspapers, and terrifying tales of murder, rape, and mutilation then circulating,

Faulkner said, he "invented the most horrific tale I could imagine and wrote it in about three weeks . . ." (*Essays* 177). He later told one friend, "I made a thorough and methodical study of everything on the list of best-sellers. When I thought I knew what the public wanted, I decided to give them a little more than they had been getting; stronger and rawer—more brutal. Guts and genitals" (Blotner 234).

Reviving characters from *Sartoris* as a framing device—Horace Benbow, his wife Belle, and his stepdaughter Little Belle—Faulkner chronicles the life of the amoral criminal Popeye and the sordid adventures of a college girl named Temple Drake. Other characters include the escort who abandons Temple to her fate, Gowan Stevens, a brothel Madam, Miss Reba, a bootlegger and his wife, and several other criminals. The shocking centerpiece of the plot is the rape of Temple with a corncob by the impotent Popeye. Despite the seemingly deterministic and corrupt world inhabited by the characters, the novel is a masterful combination of the gothic and the comic that serves to point out the tragic consequences of not taking responsibility for one's actions. Evil is punished but only by coincidence, in that Popeye is executed for the wrong murder. Faulkner finished the manuscript just a month before his wedding. He sent it to Harrison Smith, who wrote back, "Good God, I can't publish this. We'd both be in jail" (*Essays* 177).

As a married man, Faulkner needed a steady income, so he took a job at the university power plant working the night shift. Although it was probably managerial, Faulkner later claimed different, with exaggeration as was his wont: "I shoveled coal from the bunker into a wheelbarrow and wheeled it in and dumped it where the fireman could put it into the boiler. . . . I had invented a table out of a wheelbarrow in the coal bunker. . . . On these nights, between 12 and 4, I wrote *As I Lay Dying* in six weeks, without changing a word. I sent it to Smith and wrote him that by it I would stand or fall" (*Essays* 177-78). Whatever the truth about its composition, again he realized that he had done something special, a work that would compare favorably with *The Sound and the Fury*.

Faulkner had used four narrators to tell the story of the Compson family. Here he would use up to fifteen to tell the story in fifty-nine

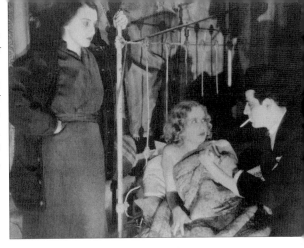

monologues of a family at the other end of the social scale, the Bundrens, poor-white dirt farmers who barely make a living because the father, Anse, believes that if he ever breaks into a sweat, he will die. It is the death of his wife Addie, a former school teacher, that occasions the action, an epic effort to return her body to her home town for burial with every natural and unnatural disaster standing in the way. Faulkner said, "I took this family and subjected them to the two greatest catastrophes which man can suffer—flood and fire . . ." (*University* 82). He compounds the serio-comic plot by revealing at the end that Anse made the difficult journey less out of respect for Addie than a desire to acquire a new set of false teeth and find another wife. The novel is a mythic comedy and a tour de force on a grand scale that only a genius could produce.

Faulkner had always been a great admirer of the major short-story writers—Chekhov, Hawthorne, Poe, and especially Sherwood Anderson. Early on he began to send out stories to the national periodicals and collected over the years for his labors a steady stream of rejection slips. In exasperation, he once confessed to an editor at *Scribner's* magazine in December 1928, "I am quite sure that I have no feeling for short stories; that I shall never be able to write them, yet for some strange reason I continue to do so, and to try them on *Scribner's* with unflagging optimism" (*Letters* 42). Finally, a little over a year later, *The Forum* magazine accepted and published "A Rose for Emily" in its issue for April 1930. His very first short story in a major periodical would prove to be his best known, most frequently anthologized, and critically acclaimed piece of fiction outside the novels. Its importance for the moment was that it opened the way for him to pursue another source of income, and as his career and reputation prospered, he eventually found himself sought after by the large circulation magazines, such as *The Saturday Evening Post, Harper's, Scribner's, The Atlantic Monthly,* and *Story.*

While the stories would bring in only a few hundred dollars each, there was a major need for new income at the moment as Faulkner had decided to become a homeowner. When Oxford was just a frontier settlement in the 1840s, an Irish planter named Robert B. Shegog arrived by way of Tennessee determined to establish an estate that would eventually encompass 6,000 acres and almost ninety slaves. As would the fictional character Thomas Sutpen in *Absalom, Asbsalom!,* Shegog decided in 1844 to erect a home worthy of his new position in the woods near Oxford with slave labor and a local carpenter named William Turner (myth would make him an English architect, just as Sutpen would import a French architect to build his mansion in the novel). The home had passed through several hands and was known as the Bailey Place when Faulkner was offered the house at $6,000 with no down payment and a 6% loan repaid at $75 a month.

On April 12, 1930, he signed the papers for the badly deteriorated house. It had no electricity or plumbing but came with four acres of land, a brick smokehouse, a barn, and servants' quarters. As lots became available to the east, he bought additional land until his holdings became over thirty-one acres. It took more than ten years to restore and renovate the house, but when it was finished, the four wooden columns supporting the Grecian roof, the balcony, and the Georgian front door gave it the appearance of a mansion, although of a modest design inside. Once more the Faulkners had a home commensurate with their former status in Oxford.

Faulkner took pride in renaming it Rowan Oak out of Sir James Frazer's *The Golden Bough,* which retold the legend of the Rowan

Above, Rowan Oak in 1973.
Below, an old oak tree and woods near Rowan Oak where Faulkner and friends frequently hunted.

A young journalist-photographer from Memphis, Marshall J. Smith, turned up unannounced at Rowan Oak in the summer of 1931. Faulkner not only allowed him to take photographs, he also played along with his current notoriety over *Sanctuary* by appearing with a corncob pipe, cultivating his farm crops, and entering the outhouse with a newspaper in hand.

Faulkner plays with his daughter Jill on the front steps at Rowan Oak in the winter after her birth in 1933.

trees thought by the Celts to provide security and peace and protection from evil spirits. He settled in with a less-than-happy Estelle and her two children by her first marriage, Victoria and Malcolm. On January 11, 1931, their first child together was born, named Alabama, but she survived only nine days. Faulkner would forever mourn her loss. Their second daughter, Jill, was born July 24, 1933, and she promptly became his "heart's darling," as he had called his fictional daughter Caddie in *The Sound and the Fury*. At one time or another, Rowan Oak had as many as four children living there, including Faulkner's niece Dean. Reportedly he created a ghost story about a Judith Shegog who threw herself from the balcony when she was rejected by her lover and was buried beneath a Magnolia tree in the garden. The intention, besides amusing them, was to keep the children off the dangerous balcony.

As I Lay Dying was published on October 6, 1930. Many reviewers were unsettled by the nitty-gritty details of the Bundrens' shabby way of life and some of the repulsive details of the novel, such
as a rotting corpse, not to mention the style that borders on surre-
alism, or even what would become known as magic realism. Most
of them, however, recognized the technical brilliance of the work
and agreed with Ted Robinson in his review for the Cleveland *Plain
Dealer* that Faulkner was "one of the two or three original geniuses of our generation" (October 12, 1930). No doubt, Faulkner was
also pleased to hear warm praise from English reviewers on the
publication of the British edition of *Soldiers' Pay* in June of that
year. Novelist Arnold Bennett wrote, "Faulkner is the coming man.
He has inexhaustible invention, powerful imagination, a wondrous
gift of characterization, a finished skill in dialogue; and he writes
generally like an angel" (Blotner 263). Another reviewer ranked
him above Ernest Hemingway and D. H. Lawrence.

What he really needed now more than praise was money, as Rowan
Oak drained all his existing resources. It was time to return to his
admittedly salacious potboiler *Sanctuary* and see what could be done
to redeem it but maintain its calculated popular appeal. The truth is, it
was never the piece of trash Faulkner pretended it was all along, but
when the galley proofs arrived in mid-November of 1930, he saw that it

needed work. The publisher apparently had changed his mind about publishing the novel and was willing to take the risk of public condemnation if it would turn a profit. Since rewriting the novel in galley proof entailed extra charges by the printer, Faulkner agreed to share the expense with Harrison Smith. What emerged as Faulkner rewrote and reorganized the novel is a remarkable blend of modernist literary impulses in the tradition of T. S. Eliot's *The Waste Land* and the hard-boiled film noir tradition of popular literature and motion pictures. French author Andre Malraux would say that *Sanctuary* demonstrated "the intrusion of Greek tragedy into the detective story" (Blotner 276). All the violence remained—including the bizarre rape by corncob and at least nine murders—but the structure of the novel worked better. Faulkner later reported that he wanted to make something out of it that would not shame *The Sound and the Fury* and *As I Lay Dying*, and later critical opinion would support his success.

Sanctuary was published on February 9, 1931, and within a month sold 3,519 copies, more than *The Sound and the Fury* and *As I Lay Dying* combined. It also received twice as many reviews as any of the previous books. Even some of Faulkner's most ardent supporters couldn't take the novel's brutality—Ted Robinson in the Cleveland *Plain Dealer*, for example, called it "obscenely diabolical" (February 8, 1931)—but one result of the notoriety in the press was that Faulkner came to the attention of many critics who previously had felt it safe to ignore him as a promising writer not yet in full stride. It was with *Sanctuary* that Faulkner became identified with the school of Naturalism—through the comments of such critics as Henry Seidel Canby (*Saturday Review of Literature*, March 21, 1931) and Alan Reynolds Thompson (*Bookman*, April, 1931)—a mistaken notion that it would take another decade of writing and finally some overt statements on the part of the author, especially the Nobel Prize Address, to eradicate. One story told in Oxford held that when Faulkner's father saw a university coed carrying a copy of

Sanctuary, he stopped her and told her that it wasn't fit for her to read. Almost a decade later, Faulkner would comment, "I'll always be known as the corncob man" (Blotner 400).

In the hopes of raising funds, the mailing and re-mailing of short stories had been hot and heavy since purchasing Rowan Oak. Faulkner kept an elaborate submission chart of which manuscripts were where to avoid sending a story to the same magazine twice. Some of his best stories were seeing print slowly but surely—"Red Leaves," "Dry September," "Lizards in Jamshyd's Courtyard," "Spotted Horses,"

WILLIAM C. FAULKNER

"Hair," and "That Evening Sun," the last a prequel to *The Sound and the Fury* featuring the Compson children. Therefore he proposed the idea of a collection of short stories to Harrison Smith, who accepted and published them as *These 13* on September 21, 1931. Probably coasting on the notoriety of *Sanctuary*, it outsold every other book of Faulkner's except that one. Except for two or three unfavorable reviews—most notably one in *The Nation* (November 2, 1931) by Lionel Trilling, who believed Faulkner's work was too frequently minor—*These 13* was warmly received, and the critics repeated a litany of praise for the writer as a major American talent, possessed perhaps by a moody spirit of gothic despair but brilliantly versatile in style and technique.

Good things were happening in small but conclusive ways that buttressed his growing reputation. The prestigious Gallimard publishing house acquired the rights to translate *As I Lay Dying* and *Sanctuary* into

Portrait of Faulkner an two illustra by comic b artist André Juillard for French editi As I Lay Dy translated b Maurice-Ed Coindreau Tandis que j'agonise.

French, which would bring Faulkner into contact with his brilliant translator Maurice Edgar Coindreau, who would prove primarily responsible for his high reputation abroad. The first American writer to receive the Nobel Prize in Literature, Sinclair Lewis, praised Faulkner in his acceptance speech in Stockholm in December 1930. In the kind of treatment accorded major writers, special limited editions began to appear: *Idyll in the Desert*, a signed edition of a short story issued by Random House in 1931; *Salmagundi*, a collection of articles and poems Faulkner contributed to *The Double Dealer* and *The New Republic* when in New Orleans, published in May, 1932, by a Milwaukee bookstore owner named Paul Romaine; and *Miss Zilphia Grant*, a signed edition of a short story originally submitted to *The Southwest Review*, published in 300 copies by the Book Club of Texas on June 27, 1932, with an appreciative introduction by Professor Henry Nash Smith. Smith had the distinction of being the only professor to lose his job over writing about Faulkner. Southern Methodist University forced him to resign for interviewing and associating himself with an obscene writer. He went on to a distinguished career as a founder of the myth and symbol school of criticism in the American studies movement.

When James Southall Wilson, a professor at the University of Virginia, decided to organize a meeting of distinguished Southern writers, the list of people to be invited included Faulkner, as well as Ellen Glasgow, James Branch Cabell, Thomas Wolfe, Sherwood Anderson, Allen Tate, Donald Davidson, Julia Peterkin, Paul Green, DuBose Heyward, and Laurence Stallings, nearly everyone who was anyone on the roster of writers who were creating what would become known as the Southern Literary Renaissance. While Faulkner would prove to be the leading light in that development, he was not one given to joining literary groups, coteries, or fellowships of the sort that had fostered the Fugitive poets, the Nashville Agrarians, or the lost generation writers who gathered around Gertrude Stein in Paris after World War I. Nevertheless, he agreed to come for the October meeting, no doubt encouraged by the free roundtrip ticket that would bring him to New York afterwards and spending money provided by his publisher, Harrison Smith.

Faulkner warned Wilson that he was not a sociable person but was rather like the hound dog that hid under a wagon on the town square: "He might be cajoled or scared out for a short distance, but first thing you know he has scuttled back under the wagon; maybe he growls at you a little. Well, that's me" (*Letters* 51). But Faulkner would do a good deal more than stay quiet in a corner. He proceeded to maintain throughout the beginning discussions a slight alcoholic buzz, disappeared from time to time with a drink in hand, and crooned "Carry Me Back to Old Virginny" in the back seat of a car carrying him to dinner. Stories of his conduct became legend, including what was said to him by the Virginia writer Amelie Rives, through whose nearby house he carelessly wandered: "Mr. Faulkner, I have seen how you have walked through my house and looked through my rooms, but I've forgiven you because you were accompanied by genius" (Blotner 286).

When he arrived in New York, the word was that Harrison Smith was in financial trouble and several other publishers were vying to sign up Faulkner for their lists. To prevent this, Smith sent Faulkner on a trip to Florida and North Carolina, but things got worse on his return. Finally Smith set up another firm called Harrison Smith and Robert Haas and took his staff and Faulkner with him. The author stood by the man who had faithfully supported and seen into print some of his best books. The next novel would add to that impressive list, but before Faulkner could focus on that manuscript which was in progress, he took advantage of what New York had to offer in terms of useful contacts.

Two agents from Hollywood talked to him about writing for the film industry, and reportedly Tallulah Bankhead, originally from Alabama, approached him to write a script for her. He is supposed to have replied, "I'd like to help a Southern girl who's climbing to the top. But you're too pretty and nice a girl to play in anything *I'd* write" (Blotner 289). Either he was uninformed or being sarcastic, since she had already made a name for herself playing tarts and shady women. Faulkner met Dorothy Parker, who greatly admired him, and through her he came to know other members of the Algonquin round table group of wits and critics. He also met H. L. Mencken, Robert Benchley, John O'Hara, John Dos Passos, Nathaniel West, Dashiell Hammett, Lillian Hellman, and Bennet Cerf. Stories of rudeness and drunkenness abounded, as when Faulkner told a prominent publisher at a party who asked him to autograph a set of his books, "I only sign books for my friends" (Blotner 294). All of the attention and parties led him to write Estelle, with unusual immodesty, "I have created a sensation. . . . In fact, I have learned with astonishment that I am now the most important figure in American letters" (*Letters* 53-54). Finally the drinking got out of hand, and Estelle came to New York to retrieve him, but not before she too partook of several rounds of parties and drinking and left behind a few tales of her own misbehavior, including a threat to throw herself out of a window in the presence of Dorothy Parker.

Back in Oxford in time for Christmas of 1931, Faulkner got out a manuscript called "Dark House" which he had begun the previous August and worked on in brief periods of time throughout his recent travels. By February of 1932 he had finished the first draft and in March sent the revised typescript to Harrison Smith under the title *Light in August*. Before the book would see print, another entirely new round of experiences greeted Faulkner that year. His discussions, while in New York, with agents from Hollywood resulted in an offer of a screenplay contract at $500 a week for six weeks from MGM Studios, the leading American film producer at that time. Strapped for cash as usual, he took the offer and headed for Hollywood by train to report for work by May 7.

Almost from day one the Faulkner tales began. He arrived at the studio cut and bleeding, apparently having been drinking. When he was told to work on a Wallace Beery film about wrestling, he said he wanted to write for Mickey Mouse movies. He promptly disappeared for a week but finally settled down to produce a script indirectly based on one of his own unsold short stories. While unusable, it reflected the fact that Faulkner was learning to write for the screen. He worked hard in the following weeks and produced a remarkable number of scripts, but none of them clicked, so his contract was concluded. Just as he prepared to leave for home, he met producer Howard Hawks, who was an admirer of his fiction, and the two became fast friends.

His association with Hawks generated another widely repeated story about the time Hawks took Faulkner along on a hunting trip with Clark Gable. The conversation turned to literature, and Gable is supposed to have asked Faulkner who were the greatest living

Publicity still from the film Today We Live *released in 1933 by Metro-Goldwyn-Mayer. Faulkner wrote the script based on his own short story, "Turnabout," at the request of Howard Hawks. The cast featured Franchot Tone, Joan Crawford, and Robert Young.*

writers. Faulkner listed Hemingway, Willa Cather, Thomas Mann, John Dos Passos, and himself. Gable responded, "Oh. Do you write?" "Yes, Mr. Gable," Faulkner responded, "What do you do?" (Blotner 309-10). If it happened, it probably had to do more with wit and sarcasm than ignorance on the part of either.

Hawks had optioned Faulkner's story "Turnabout" and wanted to hire him to write the script, so he returned to the MGM payroll. Although he was forced to rewrite the all-male story to include a role for a woman, specifically contract player Joan Crawford, Faulkner turned out a first-rate script that became an admired and popular film, *Today We Live*. The script harked back to themes developed as early as *The Sound and the Fury*. Despite this success, he could not remain in Hollywood, as word came on August 7 that Faulkner's father had died of a heart attack. Now the remaining family members depended on Bill entirely for survival.

The new firm of Harrison Smith and Robert Haas published *Light in August* on October 6, 1932. Given Faulkner's high reputation and the major accomplishments behind him, one might have expected the critics to have been better prepared for what many consider another masterwork. Several of them, however, were unsettled by what appeared to be a disjointed plot structure that failed to combine the separate stories of Lena Grove and Joe Christmas, by the frank treatment of social attitudes in the South on the subject of miscegenation, by the sensational depiction of prostitution and sexual perversion in sordid detail, and by the portrayal of the violence of decapitation and castration. Yet most of the reviews tended to be favorable and their authors realized that this was not simply another chapter in Faulkner's history of the decline and fall of the South but a novel that touched on philosophic and social issues of broad relevance. In his treatment of the irrational reactions of man to the categories of race and color, Faulkner was ahead of his time. No other writer had dared explode the stereotype of the tragic mulatto in such a fashion. More important, however, he used racial identity as a metaphor to represent self-understanding in an increasingly disoriented world and thereby posited a situation of universal application. A financial boost came in the form of $6,000 Faulkner received from Paramount Studios for the film rights to *Sanctuary*, which would be released in May of the following year as *The Story of Temple Drake* with Miriam Hopkins in the title role.

At the beginning of 1933, Faulkner took time away from Hollywood as often as he could. Returning to his old passion, he took flying lessons in Memphis from a veteran pilot and flying circus stuntman named Captain Vernon C. Omlie. Along with his wing-walking wife, Phoebe, the Omlies would serve as models for characters in the novel *Pylon*. Faulkner finally soloed on April 20 in a Waco biplane, but it took him more time than most students, and landing would remain a problem. Nevertheless, by December, he had his pilot's license. He also returned to another passion— poetry. Drawing together the public and private poems he had been writing since 1919, many in pursuit of love affairs, he grouped the poems according to moods and methods and submitted the collection to Harrison Smith. It appeared as *A Green Bough* on April 20, 1933, the same day he flew solo for the first time.

Faulkner in 1934, happy o[ ] having just purchased his own Waco biplane.

If the plane gave him wings, the reviewers of his poetry did not. Taking into account his standing by now as a novelist of undeniable power, it is little wonder that the critics were taken aback by the ordinary quality of this poetry collection. It seems clear that the only reason the book received the attention it did was that Faulkner the novelist had written it. Everyone felt obliged to call the poetry derivative, and among the names mentioned were Tennyson, Housman, Heine, Eliot, H.D., and Aiken—no surprises there. As the reviewer for the Cincinnati *Times-Star* put it, through the book "one may sketchily trace the history of English poetry from E. E. Cummings back to Marlowe or Johnson" (April 25, 1933). Perhaps publishing the book served as a purgative for Faulkner, who never again nurtured the notion of being a poet.

Faulkner would remain nostalgic about the possibility, however. As he later told a group of students at the University of Virginia, "I've often thought that I wrote the novels because I found I couldn't write the poetry, that maybe I wanted to be a poet, maybe I think of myself as a poet, and I failed at that, I couldn't write the poetry, so I did the next best thing" (*University* 4). His continued admiration for poetry showed in the explanation he gave the students when they asked him to define it: "It's some moving, passionate moment of the human condition distilled to its absolute essence" (*University* 202). Just a few days before *A Green Bough* was published and Faulkner flew solo, he had the pleasure of escorting his entire family to the national premier of *Today We Live* on April 12 at the Lyric Theatre in Oxford, where he even took to the stage to comment on writing fiction and screenplays and demonstrated that his time in Hollywood was not wasted.

With no book-length manuscript finished but with several underway, when Harrison Smith pressured Faulkner for something to put into production at the end of 1933, he gave him another collection of short stories. Fourteen of them, which had continued to earn small amounts from popular magazines, were published as *Dr. Martino and Other Stories* on April 16, 1934. The response was mixed, Faulkner's admirers seeking to find some few words of praise for an uneven selection and his detractors taking delight in citing the inadequacies of the worst of the lot. Nearly everyone recognized the narrative power and gripping style of "The Hound," and the kind of respectful care exercised in discussing Faulkner, no matter the critical disposition, was itself an indication of the reputation he had achieved.

With his pilot's license in hand, Faulkner was greatly enjoying the fulfillment of his early dream of being a pilot. He arranged for his youngest brother Dean to take lessons, and soon all the Faulkner brothers were flying. He bought from Omlie his own Waco cabin biplane. On one occasion Dean, Faulkner, and Omlie flew to New York so that Faulkner could meet with his publisher. In February of 1934, they flew to New Orleans for the grand opening of the Shushan Airport featuring races, stunt flying, and the raucous celebration of Mardi Gras. Any number of mishaps and tragedies plagued the aerial events with crashed planes and lost lives, but Faulkner, when he wasn't drunk, was intrigued by the foolhardy souls who courted death in the pursuit of speed and mechanical excess. Back home in the spring, he even mounted with Dean and Omlie his own air show billed in circulars as "William Faulkner's (Famous Author) Air Circus" (Blotner 330). All of this would feed into a novel which Faulkner wrote in the last two months of 1934 and which would appear three months later on March 25, 1935, as *Pylon*.

If the two preceding books failed by and large to please the reviewers, this one pleased them even less. The hostility that discreetly lurked behind the demeanor of Faulkner's sharpest critics burst into outright slander. For instance, Sterling North in the Chicago *Daily News* wrote, "Faulkner's new book is a sloppy, disgusting, nauseating performance by a half-articulate southerner who

A 1936 photograph of Faulkner dressed like Charlie Chaplan's Tramp as a country gentleman.

never entirely learned his job as a novelist and, aside from a few short stories and parts of *Light in August*, is a second-rater" (March 27, 1935). In that the plot moved entirely outside the Yoknapatawpha cycle of fiction, which had earned him prominence, the book created problems for even his staunchest admirers. The disillusioned barnstormers who wander through the story, told by a cynical reporter were closer to the inhabitants of Eliot's *The Waste Land* than the decadent Southern aristocrats and stoic peasants of Faulkner's best work. Even John Crowe Ransom, who had applauded his earlier efforts, now noted in the Nashville *Banner* that "it is such a bad book that it seems to mark the end of William Faulkner" (March 24, 1935). Ironically, *Pylon* came just as Faulkner was receiving wider press than for any of his previous books. A few reviewers did look beyond the novel's weaknesses to detect the hand of a better than average novelist at work, and Faulkner had the satisfaction of seeing *Pylon* reach the best-seller list in spite of the critical hostility.

Almost as if in response to those critics who bemoaned his desertion of things Southern, Faulkner returned to a manuscript on which he had been working for over a year, and another year would be required to complete it. This one would deal with a grand figure like Robert Shegog, who built his house and carved his estate out of the Oxford wilderness, except his fictional counterpart, Thomas Sutpen, would sell his soul like Faustus to establish a dynasty only to watch it fall through arrogant pride and racial prejudice. It would deal with rape, incest, miscegenation, and fratricide, but in the context of a tragic drama of Aeschylean proportions. In narrative technique and symbolic power, it would prove to be another masterwork, certainly the equal of *The Sound and the Fury* and *As I Lay Dying*. Taking its cue from Biblical themes incorporated therein, it was titled *Absalom, Absalom!* and would resubstantiate his claim as a major force in American fiction.

The novel was published on October 26, 1936, in a printing of 6,000 with a signed edition of 300. It reprinted twice, bringing into print a total of over 10,000 copies. It also marked the start of a new publishing relationship since it was issued by Random House, which was run by Bennett Cerf. For years Cerf had hoped to lure Faulkner to join his list, but in his dogged loyalty to Harrison Smith,

Faulkner refused. Cerf accomplished his goal eventually by buying the Smith and Haas firm outright and hiring the partners to work for him. Every Faulkner book hereafter would be published under the Random House imprint.

As closely focused on the South as any of his Yoknapatawpha fiction, *Absalom, Absalom!* garnered more unreservedly enthusiastic reviews than any of Faulkner's previous works. Of course, a few naysayers persisted, a minor chorus led most prominently by the arbiter of the book club set, Clifton Fadiman, who confessed in *The New Yorker* that Faulkner was beyond his grasp and concluded that *Absalom, Absalom!* marked the "final blowup of what was once a remarkable, if minor, talent" (October 31, 1936). Fadiman was effectively drowned out by the unabashed adulation of scores of reviewers from all corners of the book world. Lengthy, analytic reviews became the order of the day, assessments that took into account Faulkner's past achievements and grappled for comparisons, analogues, and a critical vocabulary equal to the task of evaluating the novel. While a few critics tried to ride the fence, most made up their minds decisively, and the favorable reviews outnumbered the unfavorable two to one.

While the novel was in progress, Faulkner was living out a life possessed by its own demons and tragic circumstances. He had passed ownership of the Waco plane to Dean, who clearly was the best pilot of the Faulkner brothers. Dean met an attractive young woman named Louise Hale, who was equally fascinated by the flying culture, and they secretly married to the delight of everyone when they broke the news. Soon she was pregnant, and Dean was making a precarious living with charter flights, air shows, and giving flying lessons. Then on November 16, 1936, he was flying a group of local people who wanted to see their farms from the air when the plane crashed. There were no survivors. The entire family grieved for the loss of a favorite son, but Faulkner in particular felt responsible for all he had contributed to Dean's love of flying. He would see that Dean's widow and unborn child were taken care of all his days.

Faulkner's bouts with drinking also became more frequent, not only because of Dean's death but because things were not peaceful between him and Estelle. Their entire marriage was beset by misunderstandings, as he became more withdrawn from the world and absorbed by his writing and she longed for contact with people and some sort of social life. Estelle ran up so many bills in Oxford that at one point he published a notice in the local paper that he would not be responsible for any further debts incurred by his wife. Both drank to excess, and according to Faulkner, after Jill's birth, they had separate bedrooms and did not live together conjugally. The drinking once got so badly out of hand that Faulkner had to be committed to a sanitarium in nearby Byhalia, fifty miles north of Oxford.

Faulkner was also going back and forth to Hollywood these years, whenever the financial situation seemed impossible, which was frequently. It was there in December of 1935 that he had met a secretary in Howard Hawk's office named Meta Doherty Carpenter, an attractive woman also from Mississippi and recently out of a bad marriage herself. He courted her and eventually began a love affair that would last, on and off, for fifteen years as he shuttled between Oxford and Hollywood. Rather than offer solace, his divided loyalties and inability to commit fully to either woman only increased his unhappy emotional state. He confessed to friends that he loved Meta and wanted to marry her, but he feared losing his daughter Jill if he divorced Estelle. What would happen to Rowan Oak and his larger family back home must also have been a consideration.

Somehow the writing of the fiction continued and with no diminishment in creative power and virtuosity of the imagination. When a friend asked how he could maintain his energy mainly on liquor rather than food, Faulkner quipped, "there's a lot of nourishment in an acre of corn" (Blotner 364). In another famous

Faulkner, ab
to retur
Hollywood
another stin
screenwr
for Wa
Brothers, 1

quip, when he was in New York once to see his publisher, friends found him unconscious in a drunken stupor on the floor of his hotel room with a third-degree burn on his back from having fallen against the steam radiator. When the attending doctor asked why he did this sort of thing to himself, he replied, "Because I like to" (Blotner 387). Once when daughter Jill tried to dissuade him from entering a spell of heavy drinking, he angrily retorted, "Nobody remembers Shakespeare's children" (Blotner 473).

While wrestling with the manuscript of *Absalom, Absalom!*, he had begun a series of short stories about a white boy and his black companion caught in the last days of the Civil War and its aftermath. Written with *The Saturday Evening Post* in mind, while Faulkner disparaged them, they were invested with the themes of his larger fiction—the meaning of courage, honesty, and loyalty, and the effects of war on human values. He brought them together with minor revisions, added a lengthy last chapter, and they were published as *The Unvanquished* on February 15, 1938. Perhaps because he wrote them with a popular audience in mind, they proved to be engaging for readers of all ages.

Critics were undecided about whether to treat the book as a novel or a collection of related stories. Those who disliked the "blood and thunder" Faulkner of *Light in August* or *Absalom, Absalom!*, applauded the book for its lack of shock, sex, and perversity, while his admirers appreciated the fine writing but with considerably less enthusiasm than previous works had generated. In one odd, unexpected review in *Modern Monthly*, V. F. Calverton called Mississippi "the most backward state in the nation" and noted, "That fact is very significant in understanding Faulkner's fiction. He is dealing with a people who are inferior to all other Americans, who are living in a state of intellectual barbarism which is infra-medieval. . . . They are nothing more than the sick, stinking backwash of a dead but still rotting civilization" (March 1938). But Faulkner had grown used to irritating such conservative biased critics.

MGM Studios bought the screen rights to *The Unvanquished*, but the rumor was that they did so as a threat to David O. Selznick. If he did not bring *Gone with the Wind* to them, they would proceed to film their own Civil War epic. With the money realized from the sale, Faulkner bought a 320-acre farm seventeen miles north of Oxford to raise mules and cattle, and he asked his brother, Johncy, to manage it for him. Greenfield Farm, as he named it, would never really provide a significant return on his investment, but he could say now in all honesty that he was a farmer who happened to write, as he was given to tell intrusive reporters and interviewers.

Continuing his experiments with structure and narrative, in his next novel, Faulkner decided to tell two stories simultaneously. One had to do with an ill-fated love affair between a doctor and a married woman who pursue their illicit relationship to a disastrous conclusion in which she dies from an abortion performed by her lover. The second story, narrated in alternating chapters contrapuntally, relates what is almost a tall tale about a convict sent to rescue a woman stranded in a tree and a man caught atop a cottonhouse during the Mississippi flood of 1927. After a seven-week series of dangerous and bizarre adventures, including the woman giving birth, he finally gets back to Parchman Penitentiary and tells the deputy, in one of the great comic-tragic moments in Faulkner's fiction, "Yonder's your boat, and here's the woman. But I never did find that bastard on the cottonhouse" (*Novels II* 683). His reward is an additional ten years to his sentence for attempted escape.

Caricature of Faulkner by Richard Thompson.

🕮 Connected by patterns of escape and refuge, Faulkner said that the theme that bound the two seemingly disparate stories was found in the concluding thoughts of the doctor who refuses suicide over a life in prison to keep the memory of his love alive: "Between grief and nothing I will take grief" (*Novels II* 715). Faulkner was known to use this line himself

William Faulkner's novel "THE WILD PALMS"

—A Review by Milt Gr

Popular cartoonist Milt Gross undertook to "explain Faulkner's turgid prose" in his comic strip review of The Wild Palms in Ken magazine, April 6, 1939. Gross was famous for his wordless novels told entirely in picture

on occasion when a relationship was going badly, but it entered world culture when French director Jean-Luc Godard quoted it as a central theme in his 1959 film *Breathless*, in which the heroine carried around a copy of the novel. Although Faulkner wanted to call it "If I Forget Thee, Jerusalem," a quotation from the *Psalms* indicating the longing and pain of exile, the publisher insisted on a simpler title, so it was issued on January 19, 1939, as *The Wild Palms*.

When *Time* magazine reviewed it in the January 23, 1939 issue, they made it their cover story and took the occasion to publish a biographical piece on Faulkner by Robert Cantwell based on his visit with the author in Oxford a year earlier. This was the first of two appearances of Faulkner on the cover of *Time*, here tieless and wearing broad galluses in country style, but despite his hayseed image, no doubt the publicity helped move *The Wild Palms* from the bookshelves at the rate of over 1,000 copies a week in the beginning. In general, reviewers were understandably puzzled by the innovative structure and failed, for the most part, to find the two plots effectively integrated. It would take time and some critical ingenuity to recognize the artistic integrity of his technique in *The Wild Palms*. In that same month of January, Faulkner learned that he had been elected to the National Institute of Arts and Letters, another sign of acceptance by the critical establishment in the United States, along with the publication of highly appreciative essays by such critics as George Marion O'Donnell in the Summer 1939 *Kenyon Review* and Conrad Aiken in the November *Atlantic Monthly*, both classics of Faulkner criticism.

Not one to wait for understanding or appreciation, Faulkner moved on to the next project, which was to begin to set down thoughts he had had since the 1920s about telling the history of a poor but populous family of manipulators and soulless entrepreneurs who skillfully and ruthlessly work their way to the top of the economic ladder in Yoknapatawpha County through pure acquisitiveness. Called the Snopes family, they first appear in a short story called "Barn Burning" written in November of 1938 and published in *Harper's* magazine the following June. The story won the first O. Henry Memorial Award for the best short story published that year in an American periodical. Faulkner continued to write about the Snopeses until he had a large part of what would be the first in a trilogy of novels which sprung full blown from his imagination. In a letter to his publisher in December, he outlined in complete detail the plot and developments which would occupy him on and off for the next twenty years until the final volume appeared in 1959. He had been thinking about the Snopes clan for so long that the first volume seemed almost to write itself. It was published on April 1, 1940, as *The Hamlet*.

Less innovative in form and style than the earlier major works, *The Hamlet* was more sensational in its bawdy humor and violent subject matter, which betrayed a large part of its origin in the Frontier humorists of the Old Southwest. Faulkner had read these writers with appreciation, especially George Washington Harris and his stories about Sut Lovingood. While the book seemed to test the patience of many of his old supporters and slowly but surely to earn a few new friends, even some of his usually puzzled and wary readers began to show a grudging respect for his obvious comic skills. But his longtime booster Ted Robinson found himself flinging the book aside when he reached the passage about the idiot Ike's love affair with a cow, or so he reported in the Cleveland *Plain Dealer* (April 14, 1940). Sterling North, of the Chicago *Daily News*, who had earlier excoriated *Pylon*, took into account the magnificent sweep of *The Hamlet* in its depiction of Southern class and type, its vivid creation of characters from the sultry Eula Varner to the indomitable Flem Snopes, and its incredible range of style from comic hyperbole to Elizabethan rhetoric, to find the book one of the "outstanding novels of his [Faulkner's] brilliant career" (April 3, 1940). Hardheaded Clifton Fadiman, as

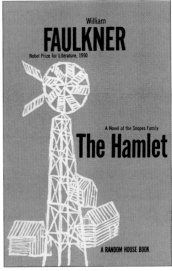

Jacket of Faulkner's The Hamlet, the first of the triology of novels about the Snopes family.

usual, had to proclaim once more, "I make no claims whatever to any ability to comprehend what Mr. Faulkner is about" in *The New Yorker* (April 6, 1940). And Don Stanford, in *The Southern Review* (Winter 1941), thought the book phony, insensitive, and stupid in its delineation of character. The majority of reviewers, however, looked forward to the further adventures of the Snopeses as they took over Yoknapatawpha County economically and socially.

Despite his increasing critical reputation and the steady flow of books and short stories from his pen in the 1940s, Faulkner continued to have financial difficulties. He was constantly pressuring his publisher for advances and trying to place his stories with well-paying magazines, often with little success. It was a dispirited and understandably frustrated Faulkner who wrote his publisher on May 3, 1940, "Beginning at the age of thirty, I, an artist, a sincere one and of the first class, who should be free even of his own economic responsibilities and with no moral conscience at all, began to become the sole, principal and partial support—food, shelter, heat, clothes, medicine, kotex, school fees, toilet paper and picture shows—of my mother . . . [a] brother's widow and child, a wife of my own and two step children, my own child; I inherited my father's debts and his dependents, white and black, without inheriting yet from anyone one inch of land or one stick of furniture or one cent of money; the only thing I ever got for nothing, after the first pair of long pants I received (cost: $7.50) was the $300.00 O. Henry prize last year" (*Letters* 122-23).

While Faulkner was reading the proof sheets for *The Hamlet*, his lifetime attendant and friend "Mammy" Caroline Barr died of a stroke on January 31, 1940. The funeral was held in the parlor of

Rowan Oak, and as she had requested, Faulkner provided a eulogy noting that their relationship had never been one of "master and servant" but rather "a fount of authority over my conduct and of security for my physical welfare, and of constant affection and love" (*Essays* 117). She had partly served as inspiration for the patient and compassionate Dilsey in *The Sound and the Fury*, but her example would also blend into the character of the steadfast and upright Molly Beauchamp, who figured in several short stories he was writing at the time about black families and their blood relationships with white families in Yoknapatawpha County. When the stories were revised and collected into a book, it would bear a dedication: "To Mammy Caroline Barr . . . Who was born into slavery and who gave to my family a fidelity without stint or calculation of recompense and to my childhood an immeasurable devotion and love" (*Novels III* 2).

There was confusion as to whether the book was to be viewed as a compilation of stories or a unified novel. It was published on May 11, 1942, as *Go Down, Moses and Other Stories*. Faulkner complained about the title, so all subsequent printings were simply called *Go Down Moses*. Perhaps there was intentional wisdom in the first title, since this prevented the nitpickers from accusing him, as they had done with *The Unvanquished*, of attempting to pass off a set of loosely related pieces as a novel. If so, the strategy had the opposite effect. Several reviewers were quick to assert that despite its use of seven stories related primarily by their treatment of the adventures of the McCaslin-Edmonds family, the volume had a unified effect and dealt significantly with a period of rapid social and economic change in the South. By and large, the book garnered more consistent praise than many of his earlier works. Reviewers noted that Faulkner's style was impressive; his range of characterization and setting, realistic; and his themes, relevant to the times. Friend and foe alike were taken with "The Bear," an initiation story that elicited comparisons with *Moby-Dick* and other classics of American fiction and that many rightly predicted would become a classic on its own.

Even before the United States entered World War II after the

attack on Pearl Harbor in December, 1941, Faulkner had wanted to support the Allied effort. He helped establish an enemy aircraft warning system for Lafayette County in June of 1941, and in early 1942 he traveled to Washington, DC, to request a military commission to teach air navigation in the Navy. His offer was respectfully declined. He would find another way to lend his support when Hollywood came calling again, with the offer of a contract from Warner Brothers in July, 1942. He spent a large part of the next four years in Hollywood, working during the war years on a variety of projects intended to help the war effort by building morale, such as writing a complete script about Charles de Gaulle that went unproduced and contributing scenes and dialogue to such war films as *Air Force* (1942) and the unfinished *Battle Cry* by Howard Hawks. He produced a lengthy synopsis for a film about the Unknown Soldier of World War I, which he described as "a fable, an indictment of war perhaps" (*Letters* 178), obviously the initial draft of what would become the novel *A Fable* over ten years later.

He began seeing Meta Carpenter again, recently divorced from her second husband, and fell into a routine of hard work and equally hard drinking with old and new friends, such as Clark Gable, Humphrey Bogart, Lauren Bacall, and Jean Renoir, who had come to Hollywood after France fell to the Germans. Renoir and Faulkner would collaborate briefly on a film called *The Southerner* in 1945, which Faulkner would recall as one of his best experiences while working in Hollywood. Following a visit from Estelle and Jill in September, 1944, Faulkner experienced a period of depression and excessive drinking that left him hospitalized. Nevertheless, he accomplished major work on Howard Hawks' adaptations of the novels *To Have and Have Not* (1944) by Ernest Hemingway and *The Big Sleep* (1946) by Raymond Chandler.

Meta Carpenter finally realized that Faulkner had no intention of leaving Estelle, as he had promised, to marry her. Although she would reunite with him briefly in 1951 in Hollywood, and they would continue to communicate the rest of his life, the possibility of a permanent relationship was clearly concluded. Faulkner's own mindset was probably best expressed in a letter he later

wrote about "the only way to get any peace out of" marriage—"keep the first one and stay as far away from her as you can, with the hope of someday outliving her. At least you will be safe then from any other one marrying you—which is bound to happen if you ever divorce her. Apparently man can be cured of drugs, drink, gambling, biting his nails and picking his nose, but not of marrying" (*Letters* 203).

With no new book out in four years, Faulkner's career appeared in a slump. Relief came from Hollywood when his publisher secured his release from his contract with Warner Brothers and

provided an advance to return home to work on a novel. Another rescue came in the form of a project by literary critic Malcolm Cowley, who had been publishing a series of major essays in appreciation of Faulkner, comparing him with Balzac and other world authors. Having edited with great success *The Portable Hemingway* for Viking Press in 1944, and noting that all of Faulkner's books appeared to be out of print except for *Sanctuary*, Cowley began negotiations with Random House and Faulkner himself to produce a similar volume. The author cooperated with Cowley, even contributing an addendum to *The Sound and the Fury*, "1699-1945: The Compsons," about which he noted, "I should have done this when I wrote the book. Then the whole thing would have fallen into a pattern like a jigsaw puzzle when the magician's wand touched it" (*Letters* 205). Because of unresolved discrepancies between this appendix and the text written over fifteen years earlier, however, it has served less to clarify the novel and Faulkner's intentions than to cause critical debate over its actual relation to the original, especially after it was published along with the novel in a Modern Library edition in 1946, combined with *As I Lay Dying*. Some view the fictional genealogy not as an integral part of the novel but rather an afterthought, or even a separate work. Recent editions exclude it.

At this stage, it was perfectly clear that with or without his books in print, Faulkner had arrived as one of the two or three top writers in the United States in the estimation of the critical establishment. For this reason, it is doubtful that the main cause of the growing appreciation of Faulkner was the appearance of Cowley's *The Portable Faulkner* on April 29, 1946, as has been claimed. The appreciation and reputation were already there, slowly building over the years, even

over for the
paperback edi-
of The Wild
Palms. which
kner wanted
"If I Forget
, Jerusalem."
dition omit-
the second
of the novel,
Old Man,"
in the theory
the two parts
e unrelated.

though a bit out of the public mind
with the lapse of four years since the
last book. What Cowley's compilation did accomplish was the orderly
establishment of a sense of the
chronology and interconnected historical nature of the Yoknapatawpha
cycle Faulkner had woven through
Cowley's arrangement of short
stories and excerpts from the novels.
Faulkner's epic intent became clearer
for the general reader, as well as the
author himself who had worked
more by intuition than an organized
plan over the years. Although it
received few reviews, *The Portable
Faulkner* did occasion a two-part
essay by fellow novelist Robert Penn
Warren in *The New Republic* (August
12 and 26, 1946) that proved a turn-
ing point in Faulkner criticism and
an influential source of basic ideas to
be developed in the following years.
Warren's review has been frequently
anthologized as a classic piece of
American literary criticism.

Writing to his publisher in June,
1940, Faulkner had noted in passing
his idea for "a mystery story, original
in that the solver is a Negro, himself
in jail for the murder and is about to
be lynched, [but] solves [the] murder

Cover for   in self-defense" (*Letters* 128). Over
e paperback   seven years later, he returned to the
of Intruder   idea and completed the manuscript
n the Dust.   in only four months. Published

September 27, 1948, as *Intruder in the Dust*, it featured a young boy, Chick Mallison, who must contend with a black man who defies the conventions of society which define him as an object or a piece of property. Any similarity to *Adventures of Huckleberry Finn* is more than coincidence, except the only traveling is to a gravesite outside town. Like Huck, Chick learns that moral duplicity and self-deception infect society, and what people say to be true doesn't always square with justice. The accused black man, Lucas Beauchamp, is labeled "a damned highnosed impudent Negro" (*Novels III* 398), who not only stands up for his right to his day in court but manipulates everyone in the community to prove his innocence without leaving his jail cell. If ever twentieth-century literature had a black character free in body, spirit, and soul, that character was Lucas Beauchamp.

This polemical novel, in the form of a detective story, attracted twice as many reviewers than any other previous book probably because of the political stance adopted by Faulkner on the race question. Basically, he asserted that racial conflict in the South could be resolved only by Southerners; that although blacks deserve equality, it would never be accomplished through legislation; and that Northerners, liberals, and reformers were doing more to damage the cause of civil rights by interfering than to help in the achievement of justice. Needless to say, such an attitude antagonized both liberals and conservatives, both supporters of a strong federal authority and states-righters. Thus the reviews were full of political polemics for or against Faulkner, depending on the disposition of the journalist or periodical. Neither his friends nor his foes found it possible to deny the power and appeal of the novel as a work of fiction, and most called the book a literary event of the first order, the New York *Times* on November 14, 1948, reporting the score sheet: "*Verdict*: Yes, by about 10 to 1. On the whole, amazingly well received, in view of the high style and the indirect defense of the South in the matter of South vs. Negro. Attacks generally from the North, and on political rather than literary grounds. Most of the attackers never got around to discussing the novel as a novel."

Faulkner clearly hit a public nerve with this novel, such that it garnered twice as many reviews as any other book to that date.

114 Courthouse Square. The second floor was where the character of Gavin Stevens had his law office in the film Intruder in the Dust.

Overleaf, a two-page spread on the release of the Intruder in Dust in the 950 university yearbook Ole Miss.

Over 15,000 copies were sold of the trade edition, and before publication, the film rights were purchased by MGM Studios for $50,000. Director Clarence Brown brought his crew to Oxford to film Intruder in the Dust on location, and Faulkner himself helped by scouting out settings and revising the script. When the world premier was held in Oxford on October 9, 1949, at the Lyric

William Faulkner   69

AW—IT WAS NOTHING . . .

COR

UNACCUSTOMED AS I AM TO PUBLIC SPEAKING . . .

BE-BEHH...

HOLLYWOOD

Como

HOLLYWOOD HOPEFULS.

THEATRE LYRIC

INTRUDER IN THE DUST

THE DARING NOVEL
NOW ON THE SCREEN!

THE CLIMA

to OXFORD !!

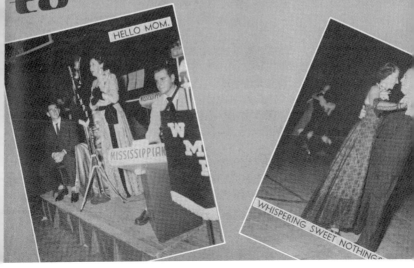

HELLO MOM.

MISSISSIPPIAN

WHISPERING SWEET NOTHINGS

Ticket of admission and program for the world premiere of the film version of Intruder in the Dust, held in Oxford on October 11, 1949.

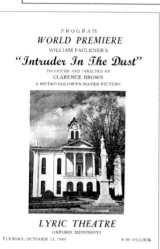

Theatre, he reluctantly attended with his family. The film went on to have a life of its own as a classic statement on race relations and was considered for many years the most faithful of all adaptations of Faulkner's novels for the screen. The author agreed and, in fact, once noted, "I believe it's one of the best [films] I've ever seen" (Blotner 508). Honors continued to come his way, with election to the American Academy of Arts and Letters on November 23, 1948, which would award him the following year the William Dean Howells Medal for Fiction, although he refused to attend the ceremony. "A Courtship" received the O. Henry Award for the best short story of 1949.

In August of 1949, a Bard College student and aspiring writer named Joan Williams stopped by Rowan Oak with mutual friends from Memphis in hopes of meeting Faulkner. She had read *The Sound and the Fury* and was profoundly impressed by its insights into life and human nature. Having won the *Mademoiselle* magazine college fiction writing contest, she hoped to learn from him. They met only briefly, but something about her youth, beauty, and eager talent caught his fancy, and soon he was courting her by correspondence. Although laced with erotic suggestions, his letters offered sound advice. While he would help other young writers, Joan Williams was the only student he would ever undertake to teach the art of creative writing. He was 52 and she was 20, but age was not the only problem as distance and personal circumstances kept them apart. The relationship would continue for five years until she met someone she wanted to marry. The truth is she needed little instruction as she independently pursued her career and developed her own distinctive voice in several works of fiction, including *The Wintering* (1971), a novel based on their love affair. For a while, she allowed him to feel once more the charm and power of passion and, as he wrote in a letter to her, be "21 again and brave and clean and durable" (Blotner 507).

There would be other women in his life—Else Jonsson, widow of Faulkner's Swedish translator, whom he would meet in 1950 in Stockholm, and in 1953 a nineteen-year-old student at the Sorbonne, Jean Stein, to whom he would grant one of his few authorized interviews published in the *Paris Review* in May, 1956. As Estelle noted in a letter to a friend in 1956, with more understanding and pity for him than anger, "I know, as you must, that Bill feels some sort of compulsion to be attached to some young woman at all times—it's Bill" (Blotner 627). But Meta Carpenter and Joan Williams were probably the two lovers to whom he had the deepest attachment, as witnessed by their frequent correspondence over the years.

Whereas *Intruder in the Dust* may have been a piece of social protest fiction disguised as a detective novel, his next book, *Knight's*

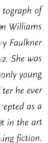

tograph of n Williams y Faulkner 2. She was only young ter he ever epted as a t in the art ing fiction.

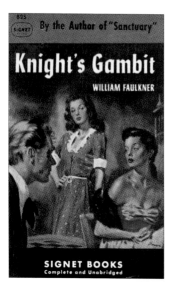

Gambit, published November 27, 1949, was a collection of detective stories disguised as a novel. The presence of Gavin Stevens as a country-store Sherlock Holmes was the only thing the pieces had in common, all but one of which had been published before, and the delineation of his character was the main item of interest. Despite the book's weaknesses, the respect accorded *Intruder in the Dust* was sustained by the majority of the reviewers, with Warren Beck in the Chicago *Sunday Tribune* (November 13, 1949) nominating Faulkner as the "Shakespeare of American fiction," and Malcolm Cowley rightly predicting in the New York *Herald Tribune* (November 6, 1949) that he would win the Nobel Prize. Even though this ultimate literary prize was only a year away, Orville Prescott in the New York *Times* (November 8, 1949) still found it possible to announce: "William Faulkner is considered by many Frenchmen and a few Americans as the most important living American writer. . . . That he is not seems to me obvious. Undisciplined gifts, intermittent flashes of blazing power, a morbid preoccupation with violence and degeneracy and a monstrously turgid and obscure style are not convincing qualifications for literary pre-eminence." By the end of the next year, despite such comments, over 100,000 copies of his books had sold in Modern Library editions and another 2.5 million in paperback.

The appearance of Faulkner's *Collected Stories* on August 21, 1950, provided an opportunity to address the question of his considerable talents as a writer of short fiction, which he had steadily published since 1930 in popular magazines and collected or revised into several books. His admirers came forward with many comparisons with other world masters of the short story, some

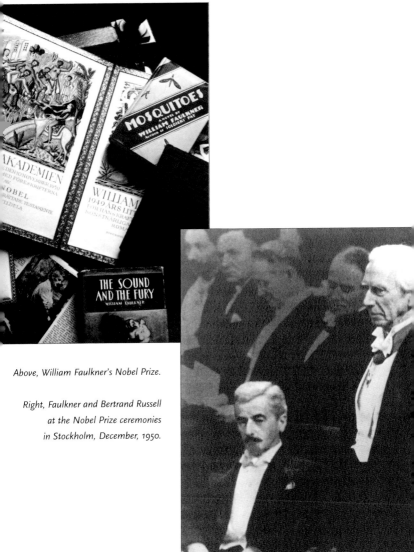

Above, William Faulkner's Nobel Prize.

Right, Faulkner and Bertrand Russell
at the Nobel Prize ceremonies
in Stockholm, December, 1950.

apt and others exaggerations, including Poe, Chekhov, James, Kafka, Lawrence, and Joyce. Even though the book would win the 1950 National Book Award for Fiction, a majority of reviewers agreed that the collection was uneven, especially for the first-rate writer who in just a few months on November 10, 1950, would be announced as the winner of the Nobel Prize for Literature.

The news came first by way of a telephone call from the New York correspondent for a Swedish newspaper who informed him of his selection by the Swedish Academy and asked him if he looked forward to traveling to Stockholm to accept. Faulkner replied, "I won't be able to come to receive the prize myself. . . . It's too far away. I am a farmer down here and I can't get away" (Blotner 523-24). He would maintain this characteristic pose of a farmer who couldn't abandon his chores throughout the following weeks of overwhelming media attention and messages of congratulation. To the alarm of the State Department and the American Embassy in Stockholm, he also persisted in his refusal to travel. He would change his mind only after his family convinced him that this would be a golden opportunity for his daughter, Jill, to see Europe.

Following a hunting trip and a bout of heavy drinking, he finally boarded a plane with Jill for Sweden. On the evening of December 10, 1950, he delivered his acceptance address in a barely audible voice. The text of 550 words, inspired by a variety of sources, including his own writings, was cited by many as one of the best speeches ever given at a Nobel ceremony. Addressing himself to young writers and taking note of the dangers of the Cold War, he advised them to dedicate their work to "the problems of the human heart in conflict with itself . . . because only that is worth writing about, worth the agony and the sweat." They must reject the fears and insecurities of those who predict the end of mankind: "I believe that man will not merely endure: he will pre-vail. He is immortal . . . because he has a soul, a spirit capable of compassion and sacrifice, and endurance" (*Essays* 119-20). The text was widely reprinted and warmly received, and those who believed that Faulkner was a pessimistic nihilist were surprised by its affirmative message. Feeling that he had not really earned the prize money, he devoted a part of it to several educational and charitable causes, especially for blacks. In 1960, he would also establish the Faulkner Foundation to give an award to the best novel published each year by an American. Faulkner was probably more pleased than he was over the Nobel Prize to receive the Legion of Honor of the Republic of France awarded at the French Consulate in New Orleans on October 26, 1951.

The Nobel Prize would act as a lightning rod, attracting to Faulkner the highest praise and retrospective I-told-you-so pieces from his supporters, and the usual vehemence from his detractors, finally to be focused on the unlikeliest book to withstand such commentary, *Requiem for a Nun*, published September 27, 1951. Originally begun as a dramatic vehicle for his friend and actress Ruth Ford, it turned into a novel in the form of a play focusing on several characters held over from *Sanctuary*. The hybrid form and experimental style confounded the purists who had resisted the lack of traditional elements in his earlier works. As usual, people like Sterling North in the New York *World-Telegram and Sun* (September 24, 1951) waxed sarcastic about the "ungrammatical, clumsy prose,"

Advertisement for the publication of Requiem for a Nun which appeared nationally in magazines, 1951.

WILLIAM FAULKNER

His first novel since winning the 1950 Nobel Prize is a startling departure from his nineteen previous works

REQUIEM FOR A NUN

$3.00 LIMITED, AUTOGRAPHED EDITION, $10.00

→ *Available in Random House Editions*
COLLECTED STORIES OF WILLIAM FAULKNER, $4.75
KNIGHT'S GAMBIT, $3.00
GO DOWN, MOSES, $3.00
THE HAMLET, $3.00
INTRUDER IN THE DUST, $3.00
THE WILD PALMS, $3.00

→ *Available in the Modern Library*
ABSALOM, ABSALOM! $1.25
LIGHT IN AUGUST, $1.25
SANCTUARY, $1.25
THE SOUND AND THE FURY and AS I LAY DYING, $1.25

AT ALL BOOKSTORES, RANDOM HOUSE, N. Y.

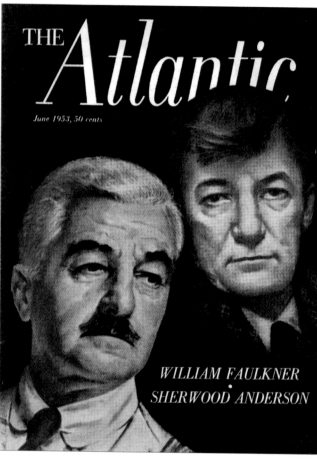

THE *Atlantic*

June 1953, 50 cents

WILLIAM FAULKNER
SHERWOOD ANDERSON

and Clifton Fadiman intentionally misspelled Faulkner's name throughout his review in *Holiday* magazine (November 1951) and recommended that he write for the comedian Jimmy Durante, since both had a genius for violating the English language. Victor Little's review for the San Francisco *News* (September 24, 1951) was a single sentence of 550 words parodying the famous sentence in *Requiem* that goes on for 49 pages. Some of the most influential critics, however—such as Robert Penn Warren, Malcolm Cowley, Irving Howe, Granville Hicks, and Louis D. Rubin, Jr.—saw no reason to hedge their enthusiasm despite the controversial nature of the work. When *Requiem* was actually staged on Broadway in 1959 as a play, the critical response was lukewarm, so it had a short run, although it was successfully staged abroad in a dozen countries.

Given Faulkner's international reputation now, nearly every major and minor periodical found it necessary to review each new book as it appeared. That meant that each would receive more careful scrutiny and considered attention than ever before, and the number of reviews would increase geometrically. The reviews of *The Faulkner Reader*, a selection from his works made by his publisher and issued April 1, 1954, were largely positive and became an occasion for reflecting on his entire career. Irving Howe, in an overview for the New York *Times* (April 4, 1954), saw Faulkner as easily the equal of Hemingway or Fitzgerald and placed him in the company of Melville, James, and Twain.

Faulkner had been working on the manuscript of his next novel for ten years, beginning in December, 1944, in Oxford, and bringing it to completion in November, 1953, in New York, using a story idea he had picked up in Hollywood in August, 1943. Faulkner more than once suggested to friends that it might well be his magnum opus. It was, therefore, much discussed and anticipated before publication as *A Fable* on August 2, 1954. Everyone rushed into the critical fray, eager to have his or her say on this most reviewed of all Faulkner's novels— more than two hundred seeing print. Given the unusual theme and structure of *A Fable*—a retelling of the Christ story set during World War I and patterned after the Passion week— extreme reactions were guaranteed.

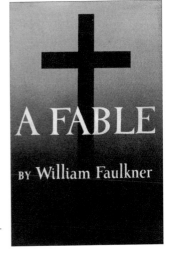

Cover of Faulkner's A Fable *(New York: Random House, 1954), his most controversial and critically debated novel.*

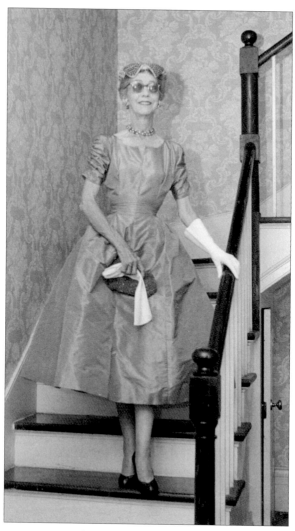

*Above, Estelle Faulkner on the stairs at Rowan Oak
dressed for the wedding day of her daughter, Jill, in 1954.
Right, Faulkner, in the 1950s, in an unaccustomed state
of mirth.*

On December 11, 1954, while he was in New York, Faulkner sat for the photographer, critic, novelist, supporter of African American music and culture, and patron of the arts, Carl Van Vechten.

Nathan A. Scott, Jr., in *The Intercollegian* (February 1955), regretfully called it "a great failure by our greatest novelist today," and James Aswell bluntly announced in the Houston *Chronicle* (August 8, 1954) that Faulkner "ought to be hanged." At the other end of the spectrum, Granville Hicks in the New York *Post* (August 1, 1954) described it as "a great novel and an act of Faulknerian heroism," and poet Delmore Schwartz declared it a "masterpiece" in the Winter 1955 issue of *Perspectives U.S.A.* Most reviews fell somewhere in between, their authors noting the presence of powerful prose but being unable to describe or define the nature of its grandeur. It was awarded both the National Book Award and the Pulitzer Prize for Fiction that year. *A Fable* has remained a novel that rests uncomfortably in the canon and in the minds of critics, its importance in American fiction still an open question.

In 1955 Faulkner drew together four of his hunting stories, including his famous tale "The Bear," and connected them with a surrounding narrative about the natural history and legendry of the South. The result met almost unalloyed praise when it was published on October 14 as *The Big Woods.* Probably reviewers were happy to see him return to the fictional territory of which he was undisputed master, or they were pleased to have a book more in the American grain, the pastoral tradition of Cooper, Thoreau, and Twain. Most agreed that *The Big Woods* represented Faulkner at his finest.

Jacket of Faulkner's The Town, the second in the Snopes family novels.

The Town, published May 1, 1957, his first major piece of writing since *A Fable*, occasioned a similar number of reviews. Because it returned to familiar territory and characters and displayed the popular brand of Faulknerian folk humor, the press was mainly positive. A few claimed to remain confused by Faulkner's rhetoric

*Above, Faulkner in
Nagano, Japan, where
he delivered a series of
lectures in August, 1955.*

*Left, Faulkner surveys
the town.*

and complexity, despite the relative clarity of this novel. But more
and more of the critical quarterlies—such as the *Sewanee Review*,
Hudson Review, and *Kenyon Review*—began to pay attention with
review essays by leading literary critics that began to establish the

Jacket of
Faulkner's
The Mansion,
final volume
in the Snopes
family saga.

critical guidelines by which Faulkner was to be judged. Because *The Town* was the middle in the trilogy about the Snopes family, it allowed for further discussion of Faulkner's moral vision and view of society.

Two years after *The Town* came the final volume of the Snopes saga, *The Mansion*, published November 13, 1959. Largely relieved to see it completed, Faulkner's supporters found many things to admire, although hardly anyone was satisfied with its disjointed structure and the distinctly political turn it took in introducing socialism and communism into Yoknapatawpha County. Paul H. Stacey in the Washington *Post* (November 15, 1959) mentioned works by Melville and Hawthorne as points of comparison and defended the structure as a "large cubistic painting put together in enormous chunks," but more frequently reviewers described the novel as repetitive, didactic, or as Orville Prescott noted in the New York *Times* (November 13, 1959), "an intolerable bore."

Despite his unease over the publicity surrounding the Nobel Prize, during the 1950s Faulkner found himself drawn more and more frequently into public occasions, interviews, and speaking engagements. It began with his agreement to speak first at Jill's graduation from Oxford High School in 1951 and from Pine Manor Junior College in 1953, requests he could hardly deny given his genuine love for his daughter. It was an appeal to his patriotism that allowed him to be sent abroad by the U. S. State Department on cultural missions to Brazil and Peru in 1954; Japan, the Philippines, Italy, France, and Iceland in 1955; Greece in 1957; and Venezuela in 1961, where he received that country's highest award, the Order of Andres Bello. Despite occasional bouts of drinking and unpredictable behavior, Faulkner acquitted himself admirably and left behind much good will and diplomatic capital.

There would be other travels as well, to New York to work on his manuscripts in progress, again to Hollywood in 1951 to work on the script for *The Left Hand of God*, and to Europe and Egypt in 1953 to write the script for *Land of the Pharaohs*, both at the behest of friend Howard Hawks. These would be his last film projects, and while he would carp himself about his time in Hollywood, he had little patience for the complaining writers who felt they were demeaning themselves there: "If they have that attitude they should stay away," he noted (Blotner 582).

It was even more surprising to find him accepting an appointment as writer-in-residence at the University of Virginia in February, 1957. Here Faulkner could be found reading from his books, answering the questions of young writers and students, and explaining to even the most persistent pedants the symbols and themes in his writing. But for one who saw him there, it was evident that he was too obliging, and there was always a degree of disdain in the way he would look through a person with his steely eyes and preface each reply with a "Yes, sir," or "Yes, ma'am."

The main attraction was his daughter Jill, who had married a lawyer, Paul Summers, Jr., in August, 1954, and they had settled in Charlottesville. There would be three grandchildren to dote on as well, and he and Estelle would buy a home with the intention of settling there permanently. Faulkner also enjoyed the aristocratic atmosphere of Virginia and riding the thoroughbred horses at the country club. He would tell a reporter, tongue-in-cheek, "I like Virginia and Virginians. . . . Virginians are all snobs, and I like snobs. They spend so much time being snobs, they don't bother you" (Inge 147). The publicity-shy Faulkner would still emerge now and then to bristle at a very personal question or, as in the case of an invitation to join President Kennedy at a dinner for Nobel laureates at the White House, he would reply, "Tell them I'm too old at my age to travel that far to eat with strangers" (Blotner 703).

There were problems throughout the 1950s as well. He and Estelle reached some sort of peaceable compromise in their marriage, with occasional periods of deep resentment. The death of Faulkner's mother on October 16, 1960, was a distressing event, and

IRGINIA, CHARLOTTESVILLE, SATURDAY, OCTOBER 6, 1956   NUMBER 15

/illiam Faulkner Accepts Invitation
s First Of Writers-In-Residence
t University During Second Term

Grant Makes Possible Series Establishment

Nobel Prize Winner Will Speak, Visits Classes During Stay Here

William Faulkner, Nobel prize winner in literature and one of America's major novelists and story writers, has accepted an invitation of the Department of English to become the first of what is planned as a series of writers-in-residence.

Mr. Faulkner and his wife will leave the region of northern Mississippi, celebrated in his fiction, and come to live in Charlottesville beginning in February. They expect to be near the University during the second term of the 1956-57 session.

The establishment of the writer-in-residence series is made possible under the bequest of Mrs. Emily Clark Balch who lived in Richmond and Philadelphia. The terms of her will provided that income from her bequest be used to stimulate "appreciation and creation of American literature." Part of the income has been used by the Virginia Quarterly Review to establish a series of prizes in writing.

WILLIAM FAULKNER

The student newspaper of the University of Virginia, The Cavalier Daily, announces Faulkner's appointment as its first Writer-in-Residence, October 6, 1956.

Faulkner walks on the lawn of the University of Virginia where he served as Writer-in-Residence, 1957.

...kner at the University of Virginia where he served as ...irst Writer-in-Residence in 1957 and again in 1958.

..., Faulkner finds the question of a student amusing ...ng one of his sessions at the University of Virginia.

...t, speaking in the McGregor Room.

Left, Faulkner discusses his work with students.

Below, relaxing before a lecture.

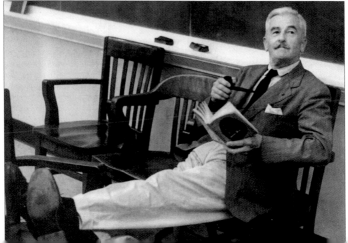

Caricatures of William Faulkner as Writer-in-Residence at the University of Virginia.

Left, by Rick Geary

Below, by M. Thomas Inge during an interview session with undergraduates in 1958.

he would miss her unfailing support. Beginning with several falls from a horse in early 1952, Faulkner would experience years of back troubles and debilitating injuries which would lead him through a succession of hospitals, doctors, and treatments, often associated with heavy drinking as well. Following extensive examinations in 1953, he would write a friend, "According to the doctor, the tests show that a lobe or part of my brain is hypersensitive to intoxication. I said 'Alcohol?' He said 'Alcohol is one of them.' The others are worry, unhappiness, any form of mental unease, which reduces

resistance to the alcohol" (*Letters* 347).
There had been plenty of stress and
unhappiness throughout his life, economically, artistically, and emotionally.

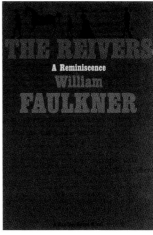

Many critics had taken note in the
reviews of *The Mansion* in 1959 of
Faulkner's statement in a brief preface that "This book is the final chapter of, and the summation of, a work
conceived and begun in 1925"
(*Novels IV* 331), and several misun-
derstood this to mean that Faulkner
was through with writing and had
completed his life's work. But there
was to be one more novel, which would indeed complete the siz-
able bookshelf of fiction from his pen—*The Reivers*, published
June 4, 1962. The publication date came just one month before
Faulkner's untimely death. His writing career could not have been
concluded in a more celebratory and fitting way, in that *The Reivers*
was a return to the kind of rambunctious and rollicking humor
that most of his readers found enjoyable.

The reviews were largely favorable. The critics appreciated the
moral vision implicit in the events, the comic elements drawing
on the frontier tradition of humor, the folk idiom of the dialogue,
and the easy flow of the narrative. They enjoyed the simple pleasure of reading about the entertaining adventures of a motorized
Huckleberry Finn who takes an automobile ride to Memphis
rather than a raft down the Mississippi and in the course of the
trip is initiated into the pains and responsibilities of adulthood.
Poet Winfield Townley Scott felt inspired to write in the *New
Mexican* (June 3, 1962), "I can only . . . record my curious sensation that I was reading a book which had long been a classic in
American literature. I daresay that's what is going to happen to
it." Willingly or unwillingly, with this performance, nearly all the
reviewers became reconciled to the idea that Faulkner was then
the major force in American letters. The National Institute of Arts

and Letters voted to award Faulkner its Gold Medal for Fiction that year, which he graciously received in ceremonies from Eudora Welty, a contemporary writer he had long admired.

In what turned out to be a highly appropriate review, called "Prospero in Yoknapatawpha," *Time* (June 8, 1962) compared the novel with Shakespeare's *The Tempest*. Little did the reviewer suspect that as was true for the Bard, this was the work after which Faulkner would break his golden pencil and retire into immortality. Following a period of illness and pain, mainly treated with alcohol, he entered Wright's Sanitarium in Byhalia, Mississippi. Faulkner died from a heart attack at 1:30 a.m. on July 6, 1962. He was buried the next day in St. Peter's Cemetery in Oxford attended by his family, friends, and admiring fellow writers.

The side of Faulkner that sought privacy and isolation often made him want to expunge himself from the public record. He once wrote to Malcolm Cowley, "It is my ambition to be, as a private individual, abolished and voided from history, leaving it markless, no refuse save the printed books," and his epitaph to be, "He made the books and he died" (*Letters* 285). But he was undeniably amazed as well at what he had accomplished. In 1953, he wrote to Joan Williams with discerning self-perception, "now I realize for the first time what an amazing gift I had: uneducated in every formal sense, without even very literate, let alone literary, companions, yet to have made the things I made. I don't know why God or gods or whatever it was, selected me to be the vessel. Believe me, this is not humility, false modesty: it is simply amazement" (*Letters* 348). In the twenty-first century, Faulkner continues to amaze his readers.

By Arthur Hawkins

*These pen and ink portraits of
Faulkner by various artists as
identified were sent out at
different times by his publishers
for promotional purposes with
review copies of his books.*

D. Parrot

*Below, caricature by
David Levine, 1963.*

Ed Bearden

Artist unknown

Jefferson, *a construction collage by*
Graham S. Frear, 1981.

Right, portrait of Faulkner by
Chuck Abrahams, 1983.

William Faulkner

Left: Faulkner's second appearance on the cover of Time magazine was in 1964 after his death in a special issue devoted to "The South." Drawing by Robert Vickrey.

Below, the cover of The American Spectator, November 1989, carried this caricature of Faulkner by John Springs to accompany a reviw of a recently published biography.

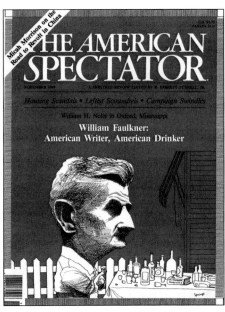

Left, a postage stamp issued in 1987 by the United States Postal Service, an institution Faulkner did not serve well between 1921 and 1924, when he was dismissed as university postmaster.

Chronology

1897   William Cuthbert Falkner, the first of four sons, born to Maud Butler and Murry Cuthbert Falkner, on September 25 in New Albany, Mississippi.

1898   Family moves to Ripley, Mississippi.

1902   Family moves to Oxford, the seat of the University of Mississippi.

1914   Meets Phil Stone, friend and mentor, and begins to read seriously under his tutelage and to write poetry.

1918   Enlists in the British Royal Air Force in Canada under the last name "Faulkner," begins training, but is discharged before graduating at the conclusion of World War I.

1919   Registered as special student at the University of Mississippi, publishes first poem in August 6 issue of *New Republic* and first short story in *The Mississippian* student newspaper in November using the new spelling of \ "Faulkner."

1921   Visits with Stark Young in New York, works in a bookstore, and returns home in December to become postmaster at the University post office.

1924   Resigns as postmaster after an official reprimand for neglect in the performance of his duties, a good deal of his time having been spent reading and writing poems, stories, and criticism. Publishes his first book, *The Marble Faun*, a cycle of pastoral poems in December.

1915   Moves to New Orleans to join a circle of writers led by Sherwood Anderson and contributes essays, poems, and stories to the New Orleans *Times-Picayune* newspaper and *The Double Dealer* magazine. Travels to Italy, Switzerland, France, and England from July through December.

1926   Publishes his first novel, *Soldiers' Pay* February 25 upon recommendation of Sherwood Anderson.

1927   *Mosquitoes* published April 30.

1929   *Sartoris* (a revised and condensed version of *Flags in the Dust*) published January 31. Marries his recently divorced childhood sweetheart Estelle Oldham on June 20. *The Sound and the Fury* published October 7.

1930   "A Rose for Emily" published in the April issue of *Forum*, his first short story to appear in a national magazine. Purchases his first home Rowan Oak in April. *As I Lay Dying* published October 6.

1931	A daughter named Alabama is born prematurely on January 11 and dies nine days later. *Sanctuary* published February 9. *These 13*, his first collection of short stories, published September 21. Attends a Southern Writers Conference in Charlottesville at the University of Virginia in October. *Idyll in the Desert* published in December.
1932	Does his first film work in Hollywood in May and befriends producer Howard Hawks. Co-authors script based on his own story, "Turn About," for film released as *Today We Live*. *Light in August* published October 6.
1933	Second poetry volume, *A Green Bough*, published April 20. Daughter Jill born June 24.
1934	*Dr. Martino and Other Stories* published April 16.
1935	*Pylon* published March 25. In Hollywood in December, begins a relationship with Meta Doherty Carpenter.
1936	*Absalom, Absalom!* published October 26.
1938	*The Unvanquished* published February 15.
1939	*The Wild Palms* (originally titled *If I Forget Thee, Jerusalem*) published January 19. Elected to National Institute of Arts and Letters.
1940	*The Hamlet* published April 1.
1942	*Go Down, Moses, and Other Stories* published May 11.
1944	Works on scripts for films for Howard Hawks released as *To Have and Have Not* and *The Big Sleep*.
1946	*The Portable Faulkner*, edited by Malcolm Cowley, published April 29. Combined edition of *The Sound and the Fury* (with the "Compson" appendix) and *As I Lay Dying* published in October.
1948	*Intruder in the Dust* published September 27. Elected to the American Academy of Arts and Letters.
1949	Begins a relationship with the young writer Joan Williams in August. *Knight's Gambit* published November 27.
1950	Receives William Dean Howells Medal for Fiction from the American Academy. *Collected Stories* published August 2. Awarded the Nobel Prize for Literature for 1949 in Stockholm on December 10, where he meets Else Jonsson.
1951	*Notes on Horse Thief* published February 10. *Collected Stories* given the National Book Award for Fiction. Travels to England and France in April. *Requiem for a Nun* published October 2. Awarded an appointment in the Legion of Honor of the Republic of France.
1953	Works in Paris with Howard Hawks on the film script for *Land of the Pharaohs* and meets Jean Stein.
1954	Continues his stay in Europe and Egypt. *The Faulkner Reader* published April 1. *A Fable* published August 2. Attends a writers conference in Brazil and travels to Peru in August for the State Department.

1955	*A Fable* receives the National Book Award for Fiction and the Pulitzer Prize. Visits Japan, the Philippines, and Europe for the State Department. *Big Woods* published October 14.
1957	Becomes writer-in-residence at the University of Virginia for the spring semester. Travels to Greece for the State Department. *The Town* published May 1.
1958	Returns for a second spring semester as writer-in-residence at the University of Virginia.
1959	Purchases home in Charlottesville, Virginia, in August. *The Mansion* published November 13.
1961	Visits Venezuela for the State Department and receives the Order of Andres Bello.
1962	Lectures at the U. S. Military Academy at West Point in April. Receives the Gold Medal for Fiction from the National Institute of Arts and Letters on May 24. *The Reivers* published June 4. Dies of a heart attack on July 6 at a sanitarium in Byhalia, Mississippi, and is buried on July 7 in Oxford.

Left, the graves of William and Estelle Faulkner in St. Peter's Cemetary, Oxford, Mississippi.

Below, statue of Faulkner erected in Oxford Square on the occasion of his centennial, 1997.

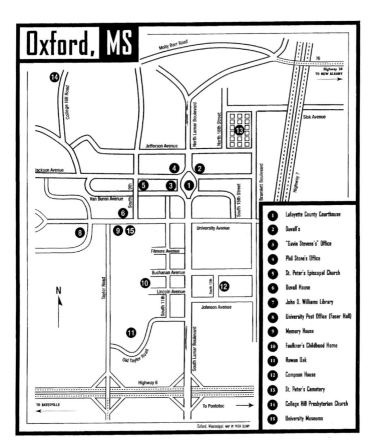

Above, contemporary map of Oxford, Mississippi, by Peter Cleary, keyed to important locations in Faulkner's life and fiction.

Left, historical marker outside Faulkner's home, Rowan Oak.

William Faulkner   99

Bibliography

WORKS CITED

Blotner, Joseph. *Faulkner: A Biography*. One-Volume Edition. New York: Random House, 1984.

Coindreau, Maurice Edgar. *The Time of William Faulkner: A French View of Modern American Fiction*. Ed. George McMillan Reeves. Columbia: University of South Carolina Press, 1971.

Faulkner, William. *Essays, Speeches, & Public Letters*. Revised Second Edition. New York: Modern Library, 2004. [*Essays*]

———. *Faulkner in the University, Class Conferences at the University of Virginia: 1957-1958*. Ed. Frederick L. Gwynn and Joseph L. Blotner. Charlottesville: University of Virginia Press, 1959. [*University*]

———. *Novels 1930-1935*. New York: Library of America, 1985. [*Novels I*]

———. *Novels 1936-1940*. New York: Library of America, 1990. [*Novels II*]

———. *Novels 1942-1954*. New York: Library of America, 1994. [*Novels III*]

———. *Novels 1957-1962*. New York: Library of America, 1999. [*Novels IV*]

———. *Selected Letters of William Faulkner*. Ed. Joseph Blotner. New York: Random House, 1977. [*Letters*]

Inge, M. Thomas, ed. *Conversations with William Faulkner*. Jackson: University Press of Mississippi, 1999.

Meriwether, James B., and Michael Millgate, eds. *Lion in the Garden: Interviews with William Faulkner 1926-1962*. New York: Random House, 1968.

ADDITIONAL SOURCES

Blotner, Joseph. *Faulkner: A Biography*. Two Volumes. New York: Random House, 1974.

Fargnoli, A. Nicholas, and Michael Galay. *William Faulkner A to Z*. New York: Checkmark Books, 2002.

Gray, Richard. *The Life of William Faulkner: A Critical Biography*. Oxford: Blackwell, 1994.

Hamblin, Charles W., and Charles A. peek, eds. *A William Faulkner Encyclopedia*. Westport, CT.: Greenwood Press, 1999.

Inge, M. Thomas, ed. *William Faulkner: The Contemporary Reviews*. Cambridge: Cambridge University Press, 1995.

Karl, Frederick. R. *William Faulkner: American Writer*. New York; Weidenfeld & Nicholson, 1989.

Minter, David. *William Faulkner: His Life and Work*. Baltimore: Johns Hopkins University Press, 1980.

Parini, Jay. *One Matchless Time: A Life of William Faulkner*. New York: HarperCollins, 2004.

Peek, Charles A., and Robert W. Hamblin, eds. *A Companion to Faulkner Studies*. Westport, CT: Greenwood Press, 2004.

Williamson, Joel. *William Faulkner and Southern History*. New York: Oxford University Press, 1993.

Wittenberg, Judith B. *Faulkner: The Transfiguration of Biography*. Lincoln: University of Nebraska Press, 1979.

BOOKS BY WILLIAM FAULKNER

The Marble Faun. Boston: The Four Seas Company, 1925.

Soldiers' Pay. New York: Boni & Liveright, 1926.

Mosquitoes. New York: Boni & Liveright, 1927.

Sartoris. New York: Harcourt, Brace and Company, 1929.

The Sound and the Fury. New York: Jonathan Cape and Harrison Smith, 1929.

As I Lay Dying. New York: Jonathan Cape and Harrison Smith, 1930.

Sanctuary. New York: Jonathan Cape and Harrison Smith, 1931.

These 13. New York: Jonathan Cape and Harrison Smith, 1931.

Idyll in the Desert. New York: Random House, 1931.

Salmagundi. Milwaukee: The Casanova Press, 1932.

Miss Zilphia Grant. Dallas: The Book Club of Texas, 1932.

Light in August. New York: Harrison Smith and Robert Haas, 1932.

A Green Bough. New York: Harrison Smith and Robert Haas, 1933.

Doctor Martino and Other Stories. New York: Harrison Smith and Robert Haas, 1934.

Pylon. New York: Harrison Smith and Robert Haas, 1935.

Absalom, Absalom! New York: Random House, 1936.

The Unvanquished. New York: Random House, 1938.

The Wild Palms. New York: Random House, 1939.

The Hamlet. New York: New York, 1940.

Go Down, Moses and Other Stories. New York: Random House, 1942.

The Portable Faulkner. New York: Viking Press, 1946.

The Sound and the Fury and As I Lay Dying. New York: Modern Library/Random House, 1946.

Intruder in the Dust. New York: Random House, 1948.

Knight's Gambit. New York: Random House, 1949.

Collected Stories. New York: Random House, 1950.

Notes on a Horse Thief. Greenville, MS: The Levee Press, 1950.

Requiem for a Nun. New York: Random House, 1951.

Mirrors of Chartres Street. Minneapolis: Faulkner Studies, 1953.

The Faulkner Reader. New York: Random House, 1954.

A Fable. New York: Random House, 1954.

Big Woods. New York: Random House, 1955.

The Town. New York: Random House, 1957.

New Orleans Sketches. New Brunswick, NJ: Rutgers University Press, 1958.

Three Famous Short Novels. New York: Vintage Books/Random House, 1958.

The Mansion. New York: Random House, 1959.

Selected Short Stories. New York: Modern Library/Random House, 1962.

The Reivers: A Reminiscence. New York: Random House, 1962.

List of Illustrations

22. University of Mississippi student humor magazine *The Scream*, 1925.

23. Collection M. Thomas Inge.

24. Collection M. Thomas Inge.

25. (*above*) University of Mississippi Libraries, Cofield Collection.

25. (*below*) Collection M. Thomas Inge.

27. Drawing by Campbell Grant, 1964. From Richard Armour, *American Lit Relit* (New York: McGraw-Hill, 1964), 156.

28. Collection M. Thomas Inge.

29. Photograph by William C. Connell, Jr., 1973.

31. University of Mississippi Libraries.

33. Collection M. Thomas Inge.

35. University of Mississippi Libraries.

37. Photographs by William C. Connell, Jr., 1973.

38. Photographs by Marshall J. Smith. Collection William Boozer. Courtesy William Boozer.

39. University of Mississippi Libraries, Cofield Collection.

40. Photograph by William C. Connell., Jr., 1973.

42-43. Drawings by Andre Juillard. From William Faulkner, *Tandis que j'agonise*, tr. Maurice-Edgar Coindreau (Paris: Futuropolis and Gallimard, 1991).

45. University of Mississippi Libraries.

47. University of Mississippi Libraries.

49. University of Mississippi Libraries, Cofield Collection.

51. University of Mississippi Libraries.

53. Collection M. Thomas Inge.

55. University of Mississippi Libraries, Cofield Collection.

57. Drawing by Richard Thompson. Published through courtesy and permission of Richard Thompson.

58. *Ken* magazine, April 6, 1939.

59. *Time*, January 23, 1939.

61. Collection M. Thomas Inge.

63. University of Mississippi Libraries, Cofield Collection.

65. University of Mississippi Libraries.

66. Collection M. Thomas Inge.

67. Collection M. Thomas Inge.

69. (*above*) University of Mississippi Libraries.

69. (*below*) Photograph by M. Thomas Inge, 2004.

70-71 University of Mississippi Libraries.

72. Courtesy Special Collections, J. D. Williams Library, University of Mississippi.

73. University of Mississippi Libraries, Cofield Collection.

74. Collection M. Thomas Inge.

75. (*above*) University of Mississippi Libraries.

75. (*below*) University of Mississippi Libraries, Cofield Collection.

77. Collection M. Thomas Inge.

78. *The Atlantic Monthly*, June, 1953.

79. Collection M. Thomas Inge.

80. University of Mississippi Libraries, Keating Collection.

81. University of Mississippi Libraries.

82. Courtesy Library of Congress.

83. Collection M. Thomas Inge

84. Photographs by Leonard J. Sherwin, 1955. University of Mississippi Libraries.

85. Collection M. Thomas Inge.

87. (*above*) Collection M. Thomas Inge.

87. (*below*) Courtesy Manuscripts Print Collection, Special Collections Library, University of Virginia. Hereafter referred to as University of Virginia. Published by permission.

88-89. University of Virginia.

90. (*above*) Drawing by Rick Geary. Published through the courtesy and permission of Rick Geary.

90. (*below*) Drawing by M. Thomas Inge. From the Randolph-Macon College student newspaper *The Yellow Jacket Weekly*, May 23, 1958.

91. Collection M. Thomas Inge.

93. (*left*) Collection M. Thomas Inge.

93. (*right*) Drawing by David Levine, 1963. Published through the courtesy and permission of D. Levine, Inc.

94. (*above*) Construction collage by Graham S. Frear, 1981. Published through the courtesy and permission of Graham S. Frear. Collection M. Thomas Inge.

94. (*below*) Drawing by Chuck Abraham, 1985. Reprinted through courtesy and permission of the University Press of Mississippi.

95. *Time*, July 17, 1964.

95. *The American Spectator*, November, 1989. Reprinted by permission.

95. Photograph by William C. Connell., Jr., 1973.

98. (*above*) Photograph by M. Thomas Inge, 2004.

98. (*below*) Sculpture by Bill Beckwith, 1997. Photograph by M. Thomas Inge, 2004.

99. (*above*) Drawing by Peter Cleary. Reprinted through courtesy and permission of the Oxford Tourism Council, Mississippi.

99. (*below*) Collection M. Thomas Inge.